CW01512094

POCKET PORTRAITS

EDGAR ALLAN POE

The Master of the Macabre

LEVI LIONEL LELAND

ADAMS MEDIA
NEW YORK AMSTERDAM/ANTWERP LONDON TORONTO
SYDNEY/MELBOURNE NEW DELHI

Adams Media
An Imprint of Simon & Schuster, LLC
100 Technology Center Drive
Stoughton, MA 02072

First Adams Media hardcover edition September 2025

ADAMS MEDIA and colophon are registered trademarks of Simon & Schuster, LLC.

For information about special discounts for bulk purchases, please contact Simon & Schuster Special Sales at 1-866-506-1949 or business@simonandschuster.com.

The Simon & Schuster Speakers Bureau can bring authors to your live event. For more information or to book an event, contact the Simon & Schuster Speakers Bureau at 1-866-248-3049 or visit our website at www.simonspeakers.com.

Interior design by Kellie Emery
Illustrations by Kim Arrington
Interior images © Adobe Stock/
warmworld, Helga

Manufactured in China

10 9 8 7 6 5 4 3 2 1

Library of Congress Cataloging-in-Publication Data has been applied for.

ISBN 978-1-5072-2413-7
ISBN 978-1-5072-2414-4 (ebook)

Table of Contents

Introduction

Edgar Allan Poe is one of American literature's most elusive figures. Since his mysterious and untimely death on a dreary October day in 1849, generations of readers have consumed the prolific works and pondered the complicated life of the famous author and poet. Poe is responsible for dark and melodic poems such as "The Raven" and "Annabel Lee," and his tales of horror are as recognizable as the author himself. Stories like "The Tell-Tale Heart," "The Cask of Amontillado," and "The Black Cat" have earned Poe the indelible title of Master of the Macabre. But you might be surprised to learn that there's more to Poe than his tales of horror. . . .

In *Pocket Portraits: Edgar Allan Poe*, you'll dig deep into the puzzles of his life (and death). Here, you'll explore one hundred biographical vignettes that peer into the world of Edgar Allan Poe, from his early years in Richmond, Virginia, to his lasting impact on pop culture. Unearth details about:

- His first poems, published when he was just eighteen years old
- His childhood sweetheart and the intercepted letters that could have stopped her marriage to another man
- How he became credited with inventing the detective fiction genre
- The bitter literary rival who defamed his character following his death
- And more

You'll also find excerpts from a number of his works, including the poems "Annabel Lee" and "To Helen" and the stories "Berenice" and "The Masque of the Red Death."

A science aficionado, a scathing literary critic, and an essayist whose topics ranged from interior design to the origin of the universe, Poe left no stone unturned when it came to his writing. He has left a lasting mark on American literature, and his controversial life and unsolved death have left fans pondering more than just his talents. Turn the page to start to unravel the mysteries and savor the literary prowess of the Master of the Macabre.

The Son of Actors

Edgar Allan Poe's parents, David Poe Jr. and Elizabeth Arnold Hopkins, were traveling actors who met on the Richmond, Virginia, stage before marrying in the spring of 1806. At the time, both were members of Green's Virginia Company, who were then playing at the Richmond Theatre. Eliza had been widowed after a brief three-year marriage to a man named Charles Hopkins.

Originally from England, Eliza came to America in 1796 with her mother (also an actress), and the young Eliza made her debut on the American stage at the age of nine. She was an instant hit! Audiences adored the beautiful, doe-eyed actress with an impeccable singing voice. Eliza secured roles across the country as she grew into her profession.

THE MORE YOU KNOW

The Boston Gazette favorably reviewed Eliza on March 21, 1808: "If industry can claim from the public either favor or support, the talents of Mrs. Poe will not pass unrewarded. She has supported and maintained a course of characters, more numerous and arduous than can be paralleled on our boards, during any one season. Often, she has been obliged to perform three characters on the same evening, and she has always been perfect in the text, and has well comprehended the intention of her author."

By contrast, her husband, David, was a law school dropout turned actor who was often intoxicated during his performances. He would get booed by the audience until he stormed off the stage in a fit of rage. Reviewers called him "mediocre," which only exacerbated his fiery temper. One evening, David showed up at one of these critics' houses and violently threatened him. Fortunately, the situation didn't escalate further.

David and Eliza traveled all over the country, performing on stages in major cities including Richmond, Philadelphia, Boston, and New York. The couple had at least two children together, William (often called Henry) in 1807 and Edgar in 1809. A third child, Rosalie, born in 1810, was rumored to have been conceived with a man other than David. Edgar Allan Poe's foster father, John Allan, referred to Rosalie as Henry and Edgar's half sister. Some believe this is why David abandoned his wife and children around the time Eliza was pregnant with Rosalie. By the summer of 1811, David was lost to history. There is reason to believe that he died later that year, but no record exists of his death or burial. David Poe Jr.'s untimely and mysterious end would foreshadow a recurring theme in the deaths of his two sons, Henry and Edgar.

January 19, 1809

I t was a bitterly cold Thursday when Edgar Poe was born in a boardinghouse on Carver Street in Boston on January 19, 1809. His parents, David Poe Jr. and Elizabeth Arnold Poe, had settled there because they were performing at the Boston Theatre. Poe's older brother, Henry, had been born two years earlier on January 30, 1807, and his younger sister, Rosalie, would follow almost two years later in December 1810.

THE MORE YOU KNOW

Today, the house where Poe was born is no longer standing. But you can find a plaque on the corner of Boylston Street and Edgar Allan Poe Way marking the approximate location. The plaque (erected in 1989 by the Edgar Allan Poe Memorial Committee) gives a brief description of Poe's additional connections to Boston.

Eliza took less than a month off from the stage after Poe was born. Her returning role as Rosamunda in a play titled *Abaellino, the Great Bandit*, was well received. Audiences were thrilled to see the beloved actress back on the stage. With both of Poe's parents working, they left Poe (who was just over a month old) with his paternal grandparents in Baltimore, where his older brother, Henry, had already been taken in. David and Eliza went back for Poe later that year, but family tradition has it that Henry remained in the care of his grandparents.

The infant Poe traveled all over the country with his parents as they performed on stages in Boston, New York, Richmond, and Charleston. Eventually, the family settled in Virginia, after Eliza's health took a turn for the worse. Poe's younger sister, Rosalie, was born in Norfolk, Virginia, and David had abandoned the family earlier that year. Eliza made her last stage appearance in October 1811 before she became too ill to perform.

Boston

For most of his life, Poe carried with him a miniature portrait of his mother and a small watercolor she had painted of Boston Harbor. On the back of the watercolor, she had inscribed: "For my little son Edgar, who should ever love Boston, the place of his birth, and where his mother found her best, and most sympathetic friends." Poe didn't exactly heed his mother's advice. Poe's roots in Boston only go as far as being the place of his birth by happenstance. During Poe's lifetime, he had quite the tumultuous relationship with the city. When asked about his birthplace, Poe would say that his family was from Baltimore (which was true), which led people to believe he was born there.

Poe would write in his editorial "Boston and the Bostonians," published in the *Broadway Journal* on November 1, 1845, that "[I] like Boston. [I was] born there—and perhaps it is just as well not to mention that [I am] heartily ashamed of the fact." Poe continued: "The Bostonians are very well in their way. Their hotels are bad. Their pumpkin pies are delicious. Their poetry is not so good. Their common is no common thing—and the duck-pond might answer—if its answer could be heard for the frogs." Poe would playfully (but offensively) label Bostonians "Frogpondians" and claim that they had "no soul."

This attack was triggered after Poe was invited to Boston to deliver a poem before the Lyceum. Poe never got around to writing a new, original poem for the occasion as promised. (According to a friend, Thomas Holley Chivers, Poe claimed he was sick and spent the time before his visit to Boston in bed, avoiding writing the new poem.) So, he read an old poem, "Al Aaraaf" and just gave it a new title, "The Messenger Star." The crowd soon picked up on this fact, and the "large and distinguished audience" began leaving one by one. Boston papers wrote, "We presume Mr. Poe will not accept another invitation to recite poetry, original or selected" because of his unappreciative treatment by the crowd. And they were correct.

THE MORE YOU KNOW

Despite his calling Bostonians "well-bred—as *very* dull persons very generally are," Bostonians today love their connection to Edgar Allan Poe and revere him as a beloved son. In 2014, a statue of Poe by sculptor Stefanie Rocknak was unveiled in what is now called Edgar Allan Poe Square, located at the corner of Boylston and Charles Streets. The whimsical design shows manuscripts of Poe's literary works falling out of his open briefcase as he strides with his back to the Boston Common toward the nonextant site of his birth.

"On the Bed of Disease"

On November 29, 1811, Richmond's *Enquirer* published the following lines "TO THE HUMANE HEART": "On this night, Mrs. Poe, lingering on the bed of disease and surrounded by her children, asks your assistance; and asks it perhaps for the last time." At the age of twenty-four, Poe's mother was dying of consumption, the disease known today as tuberculosis. This would be the first but not last time that tuberculosis would ravage Poe's life.

Many Virginia society women answered the *Enquirer*'s appeals. They helped care for the Poe children and brought the family meals and other necessities of life. Two of these women were Jane Mackenzie and Frances Allan, who each took in a Poe child after Eliza's death. The women observed during their visits that the poor children were very pale, thin, and distressed. The old nurse who cared for Eliza often fed the children gin-soaked bread to calm them down or put them to sleep.

On December 8, 1811, just months after her last stage performance, Elizabeth Arnold Poe died. With the disappearance and likely death of her husband, this left her three children orphaned. The oldest, Henry, had the benefit of living with his paternal grandparents in Baltimore. Unfortunately, the grandparents' age and financial situation made them unable to take in the other Poe children. The youngest, Rosalie, was adopted by Jane Mackenzie and her husband, William, while Edgar was taken in by the Allans (after Frances had to beg her husband to do so).

—————— **THE MORE YOU KNOW** ——————

If Elizabeth Arnold Poe hadn't contracted tuberculosis and subsequently died from the disease, it is very likely that she would have died in the tragic Richmond Theatre fire that happened just weeks after her death. The fire took the lives of seventy-two people that night and was considered one of the greatest losses of life in the country at the time. Eliza almost definitely would have been performing there that night as she had many times in the past. She would likely have been among the victims. The Allans (who fostered Edgar) were out of town when the fire happened; otherwise, these frequent theatergoers might have perished in the flames, leaving Edgar orphaned twice in one month.

————————— —————————

Poe had little to no memory of his mother, but throughout his adulthood, he maintained an appreciation for her talent and acting ability. In an article in the *Broadway Journal* he wrote: "The writer of this article is himself the son of an actress—has invariably made it his boast—and no earl was ever prouder of his earldom than he of his descent from a woman who, although well-born, hesitated not to consecrate to the drama her brief career of genius and of beauty."

The Allans

John Allan was a stern, well-to-do Virginia merchant from Scotland who emigrated to Richmond to work for his wealthy uncle. Allan partnered with one of his uncle's employees, Charles Ellis, and they established a merchant business, Ellis & Allan, in 1800 that sold Virginia tobacco to Europe. In 1803, Allan married Frances Valentine, and the childless couple took the orphaned Poe into their home less than a decade later.

The Allans never formally adopted Poe, but they did have him baptized by the Reverend John Buchanan and gave him their last name as his middle name. John Allan's financial records show that he paid for a crib and a suit for little Edgar, who was described by friends and relatives of the Allans' as being dressed like a little prince, and as a brilliant and clever child with dark curls and luminous eyes. Frances Allan (who likely couldn't bear children of her own due to her health, which was often poor) doted on her foster child. Frances's love was the first motherly affection that Poe truly knew. But since she was sick a lot of the time, Poe was often left in the care of servants.

John Allan became the keeper of the few family trinkets that Eliza Poe had left for her children, which included the miniature portrait of herself and the watercolor she painted of Boston Harbor that were given to Edgar. Other items included a jewelry box for Rosalie and a stack of letters that Allan would allude to as being quite compromising whenever referring to them. Edgar Allan Poe exhibited a lofty intelligence from an early age, and as a child, he was provided with a first-rate education, along with custom suits, pets, and other luxuries to befit a Southern gentleman. In 1815, the family set sail for England, where Allan opened an office in London and Poe attended the finest schools England had to offer.

THE MORE YOU KNOW

John Allan enjoyed hosting lavish dinner parties for Richmond's elite citizens. That was until the young daughter of one of the attendees was ambushed by a ghost! As the girl shrieked in terror, War of 1812 veteran General Winfield Scott rose from his seat, slapped the little phantom on his head, and pulled the sheet from his body, revealing young Edgar Allan Poe, who was playing a practical joke on the guests.

The Schoolboy in England

In June 1815, six-year-old Edgar set sail along with his foster parents and foster aunt (Frances's sister) on a thirty-six-day journey to Liverpool on a ship called the *Lothair*. The journey was rough. The captain ran a very tight and "penurious" (frugal) ship. The women were seasick most of the trip, and the lack of provisions forced Allan to sleep on the ship's floor. Little Edgar, on the other hand, was only briefly sick before making a robust recovery. For a boy on a long and arduous journey, he was well-behaved and high-spirited. In a letter from Allan to his business partner, Charles Ellis, shortly after their arrival in England, Allan wrote that Edgar had implored his "Pa" to tell Ellis that he "was not afraid coming across the Sea."

Edgar Allan Poe attended a grammar school in Scotland, followed by several schools in London. Those London institutions included a boarding school in Chelsea and the Manor House School in Stoke Newington. This was a rare opportunity for Poe, as many American children never had the privilege of being educated in England. Allan wrote to Ellis that "Edgar is in the Country at school, he is a very fine boy and a good scholar."

As Poe excelled academically, Allan's business venture was failing. To top it all off, Frances was always falling ill and loathed London. Eventually, Allan had to have Ellis send the funds for him and his family to travel back to America. In the summer of 1820, the family made the journey back to Richmond, Virginia.

LITERARY CONNECTIONS

The journey to England and his experiences there may have inspired the young Poe, as he would go on to write a number of seafaring adventure stories and feature England as a setting in some of his works. In his tale "William Wilson," Poe describes a school that physically resembles the Manor House School he attended in Stoke Newington. He even named the schoolmaster Dr. Bransby after his actual schoolmaster, Reverend John Bransby.

Richmond

Poe lived in multiple cities throughout his lifetime, but the city that he truly called home was Richmond. It is where Poe was fostered, and it is chiefly where he chose to be. Just weeks before his death, Poe told a friend: "I am homesick for Virginia. I don't know why it is but when my foot is once in Virginia, I feel myself a new man. It is a pleasure to me to go into her woods—to lay myself upon her sod—even to breath her air."

After his return from England, Poe attended the private academy of Joseph H. Clarke, where he continued to shine in his studies. Although he much preferred reading Latin and Greek texts over studying mathematics, which he cared very little for, he still excelled in that subject. "While the other boys wrote mere mechanical verses, Poe wrote genuine poetry," Clarke remarked, calling Poe a "born poet."

When Poe was just ten years old, he wrote enough poetry to fill a whole volume. Many of these poems were about neighborhood girls Poe had crushes on. Allan went to Poe's schoolmaster for advice after Poe asked him about having the poems published. Clarke advised Allan that Poe had a "very excitable temperament" and a "great deal of self-esteem" and that publishing a book at his age would be injurious to his already inflated ego. Clarke grasped the implications of a young boy with Poe's temperament being talked about as the author of a book.

Regardless, Poe was still talked about. He had many friends who claimed that he was a natural leader. He was charming, intelligent, strikingly good-looking, and even athletic. He enjoyed the lifestyle of the wealthy, especially after his foster father inherited his uncle's fortune and purchased a mansion called Moldavia in 1825. The mansion was situated on the corner of Main and 5th Streets, close to the James River, where Poe had performed an amazing feat just a year earlier (more on this later!).

THE MORE YOU KNOW

John Allan acquired an extensive library after purchasing Moldavia, which he stocked with books imported from Europe through his merchant business. Poe's access to this library growing up encouraged his love of reading and literature.

"Alone"

From childhood's hour I have not been
As others were—I have not seen
As others saw—I could not bring
My passions from a common spring—
From the same source I have not taken
My sorrow—I could not awaken
My heart to joy at the same tone—
And all I lov'd—*I* lov'd alone—
Then—in my childhood—in the dawn
Of a most stormy life—was drawn
From ev'ry depth of good and ill
The mystery which binds me still—
From the torrent, or the fountain—
From the red cliff of the mountain—
From the sun that 'round me roll'd
In its autumn tint of gold—
From the lightning in the sky
As it pass'd me flying by—
From the thunder, and the storm—
And the cloud that took the form
(When the rest of Heaven was blue)
Of a demon in my view—

Poe's Extraordinary Swim

In the sweltering Virginia summer of 1824, fifteen-year-old Edgar Allan Poe swam an amazing feat in the James River. The sun was oppressively hot as Poe's friends rowed in a boat alongside him while he swam from Ludlam's Wharf to a wharf at Warwick. The distance was 6 miles upstream, which made the swim even more strenuous since he was unable to rest while floating. When Poe emerged from the water after his athletic achievement, his friends wagered that he couldn't walk back to Richmond and that he would have to take the rowboat back. With a blistered back, neck, and face, Poe proved them wrong and walked 3 miles in addition to having just swam six. Poe said it was easy.

This wouldn't be the last thing Poe said of his feat. On February 12, 1840, a notice appeared in *Alexander's Weekly Messenger* about the death of a celebrated swimmer, Mathew Vipond, in Liverpool. The "anonymous" writer of this notice went on to describe a comparable if not better swimmer: a Mr. Poe of Richmond, Virginia, who was but a mere teenager at the time of his record-breaking swim. The author of this article was later determined to be Poe himself, taking the opportunity to boast about his athleticism. Poe's claims didn't stop at his swim in the James River. In a profile of Poe published in the *Saturday Museum* newspaper during the peak of Poe's fame, the writer, Henry Beck Hirst (whose source was Poe himself), claimed that in Poe's youth, he was not only a fantastic swimmer but also an outstanding jumper known to leap 21½ feet on a dead level.

While scholars today credit Poe with his record swim, many details are assumed to be exaggerations. The more the story was told, the longer the swim became, reaching as high as 7½ miles. Poe's claims that this was the most extraordinary swim to ever happen can't be verified, but his claims that newspapers everywhere picked up the story of his extraordinary swim can be: They didn't.

LITERARY CONNECTIONS

Poe's James River swim may have been inspired by the famous swim of his literary hero, the English poet Lord Byron, across the Hellespont (now called the Dardanelles Strait). Byron was extremely proud of his 3-mile cross-continental swim from Europe to Asia, which took him only an hour and ten minutes.

Jane Stanard

One of the friends who witnessed Poe's James River swim was Robert Stanard, who Poe met at a school run by classicist William Burke where both were enrolled in the spring of 1823. Stanard was five years younger, and it's believed that he viewed Poe as a role model, greatly admiring his mental and physical achievements. When Stanard invited Poe to his house for supper one evening, Poe met his first real muse, Stanard's mother, Jane.

Jane Stanard welcomed her son's friend with open arms. As Poe spent more time at their house, she took an interest in his poetry. Poe regularly sought her company after school to receive her encouragement and motherly affection. She would make him tea and lend a sympathetic ear as he grumbled about his foster father's mistreatment of him at home. (John Allan was becoming displeased with Poe's unappreciative attitude in his teenage years, causing a lot of tension in the household.)

Less than a year after Jane Stanard became a part of Poe's life, she became physically and mentally unwell, and subsequently died in April 1824. Scholars suggest brain cancer may have been the cause. Her death devastated the impressionable young Poe, and some believe that for Poe, losing

Jane was like losing a mother all over again. She was interred at Shockoe Hill Cemetery, where Poe visited her grave regularly, making sure to cover it with wildflowers. Meanwhile, at home, Poe's foster mother was constantly ill and often bedridden while he quarreled relentlessly with his foster father.

LITERARY CONNECTIONS

One of Poe's most exemplary poems is "To Helen," appearing in *Poems* in 1831. It took him more than ten years of reworking the poem to finally perfect it. In his later life, Poe claimed that the lines were "written in my passionate boyhood, to the first, purely ideal love of my soul—to the Helen Stannard [sic]." He was referring to Jane Stanard, his own Helen of Troy.

"To Helen" (1831)

Helen, thy beauty is to me
Like those Nicéan barks of yore,
That gently, o'er a perfumed sea,
The weary, way-worn wanderer bore
To his own native shore.

On desperate seas long wont to roam,
Thy hyacinth hair, thy classic face,
Thy Naiad airs have brought me home
To the glory that was Greece,
And the grandeur that was Rome.

Lo! in yon brilliant window-niche
How statue-like I see thee stand,
The agate lamp within thy hand!
Ah, Psyche, from the regions which
Are Holy-Land!

The Sulky, Ill-Tempered Teen

Jane Stanard's death seemed to greatly impact Poe's emotional state. In a letter to Poe's brother, Henry, on November 1, 1824, John Allan wrote, "[Edgar] has had little else to do for me he does nothing & seems quite miserable, sulky & ill-tempered to all the Family. How we have acted to produce this is beyond my conception—why I have put up so long with his conduct is little less wonderful. The boy possesses not a Spark of affection for us not a particle of gratitude for all my care and kindness toward him. I have given him a much superior Education than ever I received myself." It is evident here that Allan had started to resent his foster son's thankless attitude.

While Poe could be seen as a stereotypically irritable teenager, Allan's letter exposes his perception of Poe as a charity case, which often upset his foster son. (Some link this upset to Poe's struggle with a sense of belonging.) Strains within the Allan household intensified when Poe learned that his foster father was having extramarital affairs while his foster mother was ill. When Poe confronted Allan about his affairs, Allan was furious.

Allan had fathered at least three illegitimate children, who he supported financially on the sly. And yet Poe, the son that he chose (although with much convincing by

Frances Allan), was constantly reminded to never lose sight of his dependence on Allan's kindness. It's easy to see how Allan and Poe became intolerant of each other's behavior. Allan eventually decided to send Poe off to the prestigious University of Virginia, continuing to gratuitously provide an education for him. However, Poe was reluctant to leave Richmond for Charlottesville, as he had just begun a serious romance with his neighbor, Sarah Elmira Royster, in the autumn of 1825.

THE MORE YOU KNOW

After his uncle's death in 1825, John Allan inherited a large portion of his fortune: a sum of $750,000, which would be well over $23,000,000 today. With this inheritance, Allan was one of the wealthiest men in Virginia. In 1830, Allan fathered twins with a married woman named Elizabeth Wills. In his will, he bequeathed them one-fifth of his estate when they reached the age of twenty-one. Meanwhile, Poe inherited nothing.

Sarah Elmira Royster

The adorable, doe-eyed Sarah Elmira Royster (or Elmira, as Poe called her) lived just opposite the Allan mansion on 5th Street. In the early autumn of 1825, sixteen-year-old Poe fell in love with the girl next door. Elmira, who was fifteen years old at the time, was quite taken with him too. In her later life, Elmira recalled that Poe was "a beautiful boy—Not very talkative. When he did talk though, he was pleasant but his general manner was sad." The sad countenance Elmira described would mark Poe throughout his adulthood.

The young lovebirds would meet secretly in a garden near their homes. When Elmira's parents found out about her relationship with Edgar Allan Poe, they voiced their disapproval. Elmira's father, James Royster, believed that his daughter was too young for such a serious romance and that Poe wasn't a good match. This became a pattern that recurred throughout many of Poe's subsequent romances, as his reputation always seemed to precede him. Poe was known in Richmond as the orphaned son of actors (an unscrupulous profession at the time) who relied on the "charity" of his sympathetic foster parents.

Despite her father's discouragement, Elmira nurtured her young romance with Poe. While hidden away in their secret little garden, Poe proposed marriage to Elmira, and she accepted. They kept the engagement secret throughout the winter, and in February 1826, the couple said their goodbyes as Poe left for college. Poe promised to write to Elmira from the University of Virginia, which was just over 70 miles away in Charlottesville. He pledged to Elmira that he would make it back to Richmond to marry her.

—————— **LITERARY CONNECTIONS** ——————

Poe's romance with Sarah Elmira Royster inspired his brother, Henry Poe, to write a short story titled "The Pirate," which was published in the *North American* on October 27, 1827. Following his brother's lead, Poe would write many seafaring stories during his career.

College Dropout

The University of Virginia opened its doors about a year before Edgar Allan Poe enrolled on February 14, 1826. The college was established by the former president of the United States Thomas Jefferson, who served as the university rector until his death on July 4, 1826. The students were a bit barbarous, often engaging in brutal fistfights. Even Poe scuffled once or twice during his time there. Poe took classes in ancient as well as modern languages, studying Greek, Latin, French, German, Italian, and Spanish. He frequented the university library, which was a slew of uncatalogued books.

Poe's problems at the university started when John Allan sent him there with only enough money for travel and enrollment in classes. Within the first week, Poe wrote to his foster father, asking him to send money to pay for textbooks and other necessities. Allan refused, so Poe resorted to gambling to try and make some quick money. This would have been a brilliant idea—if Poe were a good card player. He very quickly racked up debts he wasn't able to pay back. Deep in winter, Poe had to burn pieces of the furniture in his room to keep the fire going.

The earliest records of Poe's relationship with alcohol also come from his time at UVA. One of his classmates recalled, "Poe's passion for strong drink was as marked and as peculiar as that for cards. It was not the *taste* of the beverage that influenced him; without a sip or smack of the mouth he would seize a full glass, without water or sugar, and send it home at a single gulp." Other students, however, recalled that Poe wasn't often intoxicated and actually had a reputation for being "a sober, quiet, and orderly young man." Whatever the case, Poe excelled in his studies, but his hardships did him in. Ten months after enrolling, Poe left the University of Virginia. John Allan traveled to Charlottesville, paid most of Poe's school debt (refusing to pay the gambling debts, which amounted to about $2,000), and brought him back to Richmond.

THE MORE YOU KNOW

It's possible that Poe met founding father Thomas Jefferson at his home, Monticello, in Charlottesville. Jefferson often invited University of Virginia students over for dinner, and Poe attended the university while Jefferson was still alive. It's also possible that Poe attended Jefferson's funeral, which took place at Monticello, just a few miles from the university. Today, you can visit Poe's dorm room (appropriately numbered unlucky 13) on the West Range of the university campus. The room has been preserved and furnished as it would have been in the early nineteenth century.

Painter or Poet?

Edgar Allan Poe was a man of many talents. During his time at the University of Virginia, he entertained his classmates with not only recitations of original poetry but also whimsical charcoal drawings on the walls of his dormitory. One classmate recalled that Poe produced these drawings "with so much artistic skill as to leave us in doubt whether [he] in future life would be Painter or Poet."

It's not exactly clear if Poe dabbled in the visual arts throughout his short life. A few artworks suspected to be his that have surfaced are in the collection of the Poe Museum in Richmond, Virginia. They include a landscape painting of the James River and a watercolor of a weeping lady. The landscape was easily debunked as Poe's work by scholars, while the watercolor is still up for debate. Titled "The Fatal Letter," it came from the estate of the artist Robert Matthew Sully and bears Poe's signature on the back. Sully and Poe were friends, and Sully even painted a portrait of Poe that has unfortunately been lost.

One of the most notable of Poe's visual works is a crayon portrait of Elmira. However, the portrait is a copy rendered by Richmond artist Nora Houston, supposedly from an original drawing by the teenage Poe. That original drawing is lost, so the accuracy of the copy can't be verified. Poe Museum founder and Poe collector James H. Whitty commissioned Houston to make this copy around 1920. If the drawing does reflect an original by Poe, it is one of the few examples of his artwork that survive to support the claims of his classmates that he was as good a visual artist as he was a poet.

————— THE MORE YOU KNOW —————

While Poe may have been a talented visual artist, his superior prowess at poetry and prose inspired several famous artists. Édouard Manet, Gustave Doré, Edmund Dulac, Harry Clarke, and Arthur Rackham are just a few of the celebrated artists who have illustrated Poe's works.

Intercepted Letters

Poe had written to Elmira while he was at the University of Virginia but never received a reply. And when Poe arrived back in Richmond, ready to fulfill his promise and marry his beloved, he discovered that Elmira was engaged to a man named Alexander Shelton!

It had been only ten months since Poe and Elmira last saw each other; why hadn't she ever written him back? It turned out, Elmira's father was intercepting Poe's letters to her and burning them, so Poe and Elmira both thought that the other had forgotten them. Her father then encouraged her engagement to Shelton, who was from a well-off Richmond family and had status, money, and prospects. While no longer available to marry Poe, Elmira became one of his most influential muses.

After his return from school, Poe briefly worked as a clerk at his foster father's countinghouse (likely without pay, since Allan was supporting him and he didn't have any money saved when he left Allan's house), but the two argued constantly. The tense relationship was a topic of many of Poe's letters at the time. By March 1827, Poe had made up his mind to leave the Allan household forever. He roamed the streets before begging his foster father for one last gift of money so that he could travel to Boston, the place of his birth. Poe wrote to Allan, "My determination is to leave your house and endeavor to find some place in this wide world, where I will be treated—not as *you* have treated me." Allan refused to give any financial aid to his destitute foster son. With nothing but the clothes on his back, Poe managed to make his way to Boston.

--------- THE MORE YOU KNOW ---------

In Poe's adulthood, he would always sign his name "Edgar A. Poe," "Edgar Poe," or "E.A. Poe," omitting the family name of his foster father. Today, you will often see Poe's middle name misspelled as "Allen" in various digital and print media.

From "Romance"

For, being an idle boy lang syne,
Who read Anacreon, and drank wine,
I early found Anacreon rhymes
Were almost passionate sometimes—
And by strange alchemy of brain
His pleasures always turn'd to pain—
His naivete to wild desire—
His wit to love—his wine to fire—
And so, being young and dipt in folly
I fell in love with melancholy,
And used to throw my earthly rest
And quiet all away in jest—
I could not love except where Death
Was mingling his with Beauty's breath—
Or Hymen, Time, and Destiny
Were stalking between her and me.

Sergeant Major Perry

I n late March 1827, Poe arrived in his birthplace of Boston with few prospects. He took on odd jobs with very little pay to try and get on his feet. He clerked at a wholesale merchandise house for about two months, likely worked as a stonemason, and even tried his hand at literary work. He then landed a job as a market reporter for an obscure newspaper. Unfortunately, the paper folded shortly after Poe took the position.

Refusing to ask his foster father for help and having exhausted all other resources, Poe decided to join the army. On May 26, 1827, Poe enlisted under the alias Edgar A. Perry as a way to leave his misfortunate life behind and start anew. He also thought that entering the army would be a good way to escape his college gambling debts. Poe listed his age as twenty-two when he was really only eighteen.

Private "Perry" was stationed at Fort Independence in Boston Harbor until his battery moved to Fort Moultrie in South Carolina six months later. Within a year, he was appointed an artificer (someone who maintains and develops military equipment and weaponry). A position of importance, it came with a doubling of his pay and a daily ration of whiskey. Poe primarily dealt with weights and measures of ores and chemicals for explosives. By 1829, he was promoted to regimental sergeant major, the highest rank that anyone enlisted in the military can achieve! With his rapid success in the army, Poe endeavored to secure an appointment at the West Point Military Academy, but for that, he needed his foster father's connections. He wrote to Allan for the first time in a while, in the hope that he would help him.

LITERARY CONNECTIONS

The scenery of South Carolina inspired Poe's imagination while he was stationed in Charleston. In 1843, he published "The Gold-Bug" which was set in Sullivan's Island, South Carolina. The story involves a treasure hunt sparked by a character's fixation on a gold-colored bug. The bug ends up being a key in a code that has to be deciphered, leading the character right to the treasure. "The Gold-Bug" was Poe's most successful story in his lifetime.

Poe's Appearance

Edgar Allan Poe is one of the most recognizable literary figures in history. The combination of iconic mustache, heavy bags under the eyes, unkempt hair, and disheveled black suit has become synonymous with Poe's look. But this is not what Poe normally looked like! Poe sat to have a daguerreotype taken on six different occasions, producing a total of eight different images. A daguerreotype was the first photographic process widely available to the public in the 1840s and 1850s. The daguerreotypes of Poe were taken between 1842 and 1849, when Poe was thirty-three years old up until a few weeks before his death at forty. The images give a glimpse into the dark, brooding poet, but there were many elements of Poe's appearance that the photos didn't capture.

In his military enlistment papers, Poe described himself as 5 feet, 8 inches tall, with gray eyes, brown hair, and a fair complexion. He was slender but carried himself with confidence and had a military gait. Sporting long sideburns for most of his life, he didn't grow his famous mustache until the last four years of his life.

Many people who knew Poe said that he had the most "beautiful" and "brilliant" forehead. His face was noble and expressive. Various acquaintances described his eyes as being many colors, ranging from gray and hazel to blue and even violet. His hair was dark brown and curly, usually parted to the side with a few stray curls falling over his broad forehead. His voice may have been his most striking feature, with its softness and slight Southern twang. He would command lecture halls packed to the brim as he recited some of his most well-known works, and a friend, Thomas Holley Chivers, called his voice "musical as Apollo's Lute." There is no doubt that the popular image of Poe is a caricature of Poe in real life.

THE MORE YOU KNOW

On February 25, 1843, the *Philadelphia Saturday Museum* published an article on Poe, accompanied by the first ever published portrait of him. The woodcut engraving was rendered from the first known daguerreotype taken of Poe, in 1842. Poe sent the article to one of his friends and commented: "Herewith I forward a *Saturday Museum* containing a Biography and caricature, both of myself. I am ugly enough God knows, but not *quite* so bad as that." Clearly Poe didn't think the woodcut portrait reflected how he truly looked. Of all the photos taken and portraits painted of Poe, he only commissioned one himself (known as the "Whitman" daguerreotype; taken in Providence, Rhode Island).

Tamerlane and Other Poems

In the summer of 1827, the eighteen-year-old Edgar Allan Poe made his debut as a published poet with a small book of poetry titled *Tamerlane and Other Poems*, published in Boston by a printer named Calvin F.S. Thomas. Poe's name was not even on the cover, having only listed himself as "A Bostonian." The book of about forty pages contains several poems that Poe claimed to have written before he was even fourteen years old.

LITERARY CONNECTIONS

One of the poems in *Tamerlane and Other Poems*, "To —," which was later retitled "Song," was likely a lamentation for his fiancée Sarah Elmira Royster, who became engaged to someone else while Poe was in college. So, this particular poem must have been written close to the book's publication, as the loss of Elmira's hand just the year before was a recent blow for the young poet.

Poe stressed the insignificance of *Tamerlane and Other Poems* in the preface he wrote for it: "He will not say that he is indifferent as to the success of these Poems—it might stimulate him to other attempts—but he can safely assert that failure will not at all influence him in a resolution already adopted. This is challenging criticism—let it be so.

Nos hæc novimus esse nihil." The last line, which is in Latin, translates to "We know these things to be nothing." *Tamerlane* received virtually no notice whatsoever. The number of copies printed has not been determined, making it hard to know how much of an audience the book reached. Scholars suggest that as few as forty copies or as many as two hundred were printed. Since Poe had to pay for the publication out of his own pocket, it's more likely it was close to forty. A few copies were given to reviewers, while one was sent by Poe to his brother, Henry, in Baltimore, where Henry had a few of the poems republished in *North American.*

Poe didn't even own a copy of his debut book of poetry. *Tamerlane and Other Poems* is a prime example of an artist attempting to get his work noticed at his own expense, with little success. Poe would publish three more editions of poetry before his death in 1849, which varied in popularity.

Only twelve copies of *Tamerlane and Other Poems* are known to exist today. While the book was virtually worthless when it was published in 1827, today it is arguably the rarest and most sought-after first editions of American literature. The last three copies that sold at auction went for $250,000, $420,000, and $662,500.

"Song"

I saw thee on thy bridal day—
When a burning blush came o'er thee,
Though happiness around thee lay,
The world all love before thee:

And in thine eye a kindling light
(Whatever it might be)
Was all on Earth my aching sight
Of Loveliness could see.

That blush, perhaps, was maiden shame—
As such it well may pass—
Though its glow hath raised a fiercer flame
In the breast of him, alas!

Who saw thee on that bridal day,
When that deep blush *would* come o'er thee,
Though happiness around thee lay,
The world all love before thee.

A Moment Too Late

On February 28, 1829, Poe's foster mother, Frances Allan, died after what was reported to be a "lingering and painful illness." No specific cause of death was given (nor can one be accurately determined today based on evidence). She was forty-four years old. Frances had cared for Poe from his infancy, and when he was growing up, she was his sole mother figure. Having no biological children of her own, she doted on her beautiful, intelligent little foster son. If not for her entreaties to John Allan, the couple would have never taken Poe into their home.

Poe's battery had moved to Fortress Monroe in Old Point Comfort, Virginia, just a few months prior to Frances's death. As soon as Poe received word of her passing, he was granted leave and rushed to Richmond but sadly didn't make it in time to attend her funeral. Poe spoke of his foster mother with love, affection, and admiration. She was his respite from his foster father's cruelty.

During this time, Poe and Allan reconciled their differences (temporarily). Allan purchased a new black suit for his foster son, in addition to three pairs of socks, suspenders, gloves, a hat, and a knife. He also used his connections to aid Poe in getting an appointment at the West Point Military Academy. On April 4, 1829, "Sergeant-Major Edgar A.

Perry" was granted discharge from the US Army with the stipulation that he find a replacement at his own expense. Allan agreed to help pay Samuel Graves, a former sergeant, to re-enlist as Poe's substitute. Poe moved to Baltimore and became acquainted with his paternal family. His enrolled in West Point within the following year, but not before he tried to follow his true passion and publish more poetry.

--------- **THE MORE YOU KNOW** ---------

Samuel Graves had a difficult time getting the money owed to him for taking Poe's place in the army. Poe shifted some of the blame to his foster father, telling Graves that "Mr. A [John Allan] is not very often sober," which was a blatant lie. This information made its way to John Allan, and he was livid. It was the final straw that broke the relationship with his foster son.

Al Aaraaf, Tamerlane, and Minor Poems

In anticipation of his second volume of poetry, Poe wrote to the well-known writer and critic John Neal, "I am young—not yet twenty—*am* a poet—if deep worship of all beauty can make me one. . . .I am about to publish a volume of 'Poems'—the greater part written before I was fifteen." In this second volume, Poe dedicated his poem "Tamerlane" to Neal, assuring Neal's attention once the book was published. While Poe was living in Baltimore, between his time in the army and at West Point, *Al Aaraaf, Tamerlane, and Minor Poems* was published by Baltimore publisher Hatch & Dunning. This time, Poe put his name on the cover.

Despite having published a book of poetry previously (*Tamerlane and Other Poems*), Poe considered this his first official volume. As with the previous book, Poe claimed that most of the poetry in *Al Aaraaf* was written before he was even fifteen. This would make sense considering that *Al Aaraaf* contained many of the same poems included in *Tamerlane*. But contrary to *Tamerlane*, *Al Aaraaf* received some notice and good reviews!

The Poe family were excited about Poe's endeavors in literature. His cousin Neilson Poe (who later became one of his bitterest enemies) wrote in a letter to another cousin: "Edgar Poe has published a volume of Poems one of which is dedicated to John Neal the great autocrat of critics—Neal has accordingly published Edgar as a Poet of great genius etc.—*Our* name will be a great one *yet*." It is uncertain exactly how many copies of this book were published, but fewer than thirty are known to exist today. This makes *Al Aaraaf, Tamerlane, and Minor Poems* yet another rare and valuable piece of American literature from Poe's published works.

LITERARY CONNECTIONS

In the poem "Al Aaraaf," Poe uses two names (Zante and Ligeia) that he would repeat in subsequent works. In Islam, al-A'raf is a place where people who aren't notably good or bad are sent when they die: a space between heaven and hell where they suffer no punishment but are not granted tranquility and happiness. Death and the afterlife would be recurring themes in Poe's poetry and short stories throughout his career.

From "Al Aaraaf"

Spirits in wing, and angels to the view,
A thousand seraphs burst th' Empyrean thro',
Young dreams still hovering on their drowsy flight—
Seraphs in all but "Knowledge," the keen light
That fell, refracted, thro' thy bounds, afar
O Death! from eye of God upon that star:
Sweet was that error—sweeter still that death—
Sweet was that error—ev'n with us the breath
Of Science dims the mirror of our joy—
To them 'twere the Simoom, and would destroy—
For what (to them) availeth it to know
That Truth is Falsehood—or that Bliss is Woe?
Sweet was their death—with them to die was rife
With the last ecstasy of satiate life—
Beyond that death no immortality—
But sleep that pondereth and is not "to be"—
And there—oh! may my weary spirit dwell—
Apart from Heaven's Eternity—and yet how far from Hell!

Poe's "Sonnet—To Science"

For his introduction to *Al Aaraaf, Tamerlane, and Minor Poems*, Poe wrote an untitled poem that later became his "Sonnet—To Science." It took Poe about fourteen years to complete the final version of the poem, and some scholars believe that it is one of Poe's most important works—a key to understanding all his writings. "Sonnet—To Science" expresses Poe's belief that scientific fact is only useful until fiction can better suit his purpose.

Poe had a lifelong passion for science that started at an early age. Growing up in the Allan household, Poe had the luxury of a telescope, and he came to love astronomy. As he became a serious poet and genre writer in his early adulthood, Poe struggled with the idea that science and fantasy couldn't mix. In many of his works, he blurred the lines between fact and fiction, creating a new genre of writing (what is now called science fiction) that beguiled readers throughout America. With stories involving hypnotism and balloon travel, Poe wove in enough science with his fiction that readers believed some of these stories were true.

Despite his passion for science and technological advancements, Poe was doubtful of humanity's progress. He stated that "man is now only more active, not wiser, nor more happy than he was 6000 years ago." One can only wonder what Poe would think of humanity now! Nevertheless, Poe never wavered in his true love for science. One of his last major works, *Eureka: A Prose Poem*, was yet another example of the scientific concepts he frequently used in his writing. (*Eureka* is explored later in this book.)

"Sonnet—To Science" laid the foundation of Poe's pursuit of knowledge, which had evolved since his early schooling in England, his short time at the University of Virginia, and now the West Point Military Academy.

—————— LITERARY CONNECTIONS ——————

In "The Facts in the Case of M. Valdemar," published in December 1845, Poe blended scientific reporting with fiction so convincingly that the public thought it was a true story! In the story, a man is paralyzed through mesmerism (hypnotism) while on his deathbed, and when he is released from the trance, "his whole frame at once—within the space of a single minute, or even less—shrunk—crumbled—absolutely *rotted* away beneath [the narrator's] hands. Upon the bed, before that whole company, there lay a nearly liquid mass of loathsome—of detestable putrescence."

"Sonnet — To Science"

Science! true daughter of Old Time thou art!
Who alterest all things with thy peering eyes.
Why preyest thou thus upon the poet's heart,
Vulture, whose wings are dull realities?
How should he love thee? or how deem thee wise,
Who wouldst not leave him in his wandering
To seek for treasure in the jewelled skies,
Albeit he soared with an undaunted wing?
Hast thou not dragged Diana from her car?
And driven the Hamadryad from the wood
To seek a shelter in some happier star?
Hast thou not torn the Naiad from her flood,
The Elfin from the green grass, and from me
The summer dream beneath the tamarind tree?

West Point

In July 1830, twenty-one-year-old Edgar Allan Poe entered the West Point Military Academy in New York. He took two French classes and mathematics, and he excelled at them all. One classmate recalled that Poe was "an accomplished French scholar, and had no difficulty in preparing his recitations in his class and in obtaining the highest marks in these departments." While Poe's academic career flourished, his contempt for military duties would ultimately be his downfall. Just a few weeks after starting at the academy, Poe lost interest in being there.

One teacher in particular, Lieutenant Joseph Locke, made Poe's time at West Point difficult. Poe and Locke shared a mutual hatred, and Poe often entertained his fellow cadets with recitations of satirical poetry, written with a "stinging pen," about Locke. One cadet commented that he had "never seen a man whose hatred was so intense as that of Poe." Poe used his witty limericks about West Point superiors to gain subscriptions from his fellow cadets for his next volume of poetry, which he would publish the following year.

By early 1831, less than a year after Poe's entry into West Point, he was court-martialed for purposely neglecting his duties and ultimately dismissed from the academy. Meanwhile, John Allan had married Louisa Patterson, the woman who would help drive an even greater wedge between her husband and his foster son. The new Mrs. Allan constantly validated John Allan's ill feelings toward Poe and discouraged any support Allan considered giving him. Poe wrote Allan a letter on January 3, 1831, that blamed him for Poe's lack of success at West Point and the University of Virginia. Allan summarized this letter with the following: "I do not think the Boy has one good quality. He may do or act as he pleases, tho' I wd have saved him but on his own terms & conditions since I cannot believe a word he writes. His letter is the most barefaced one sided statement."

THE MORE YOU KNOW

There is a legend that Poe got expelled from West Point after reporting to a morning drill naked. When the parade uniform was announced as white belts and gloves, Poe reportedly followed orders by wearing *only* a white belt and gloves. While this matches Poe's sense of humor and love of pranks, his court-martial officially stated that his dismissal was for gross neglect of duties and disobeying orders.

Poems, Dedicated to the Cadets at West Point

Edgar Allan Poe left West Point for New York in February 1831. He had no cloak or decent clothes and few possessions to his name. His West Point frock coat stayed with him for the remainder of his life, and he was photographed wearing it in both 1843 and 1848 (less than a year before his death). As promised to his fellow cadets, Poe published a collection of poems in April 1831, and he dedicated the volume to "The U.S. Corps of Cadets."

Out of 232 West Point cadets, 131 contributed $1.25 each toward the publication of *Poems*, which the superintendents at West Point allowed to be deducted from their pay. Former classmate Thomas Gibson described the book as a "puny volume, of about fifty pages, bound in boards and badly printed on coarse paper" and continued that "worse than all, it contained not one of the squibs and satires upon which his reputation at the Academy had been built up. . . .For months afterward quotations from Poe formed the standing material for jests in the corps, and his reputation for genius went down to zero."

Poems consisted of melancholy poetry the cadets were not expecting. Many threw their copies in the Hudson

River out of pure disgust, which is why only about twenty first editions exist today. The cadets at West Point were not the only ones dissatisfied with *Poems*. Reviewers deemed the volume nonsense, claiming that most of the poetry was incomprehensible. One reviewer even said, "The poetry of this little volume has a plausible air of imagination, inconsistent with the general indefinitiveness of the ideas. Every think in the language betokens poetic inspiration, but it rather resembles the leaves of the sybil when scattered by the wind." Despite all the backlash, Poe stayed the course in his literary pursuits. Both his life and his career would take a monumental turn after he moved into the Baltimore home of his paternal aunt, Maria Clemm.

LITERARY CONNECTIONS

Poe's fellow cadets at West Point expected poems such as "Lines on Joe Locke," which Poe would end up publishing in the *Philadelphia Saturday Museum* in 1843. This little poem exemplifies the type of satirical verse he would recite to his fellow cadets to entertain them. In particular, it pokes fun at the insufferable Lieutenant Joseph Locke.

"Lines on Joe Locke"

As for Locke, he is all in my eye,
May the d—l right soon for his soul call.
He never was known to lie—
In bed at a *reveillé* "roll-call."

John Locke was a notable name;
Joe Locke is a greater: in short,
The former was well known to fame,
But the latter's well known "to report."

Muddy & Sissy

When spring came in 1831, Poe started over yet again. John Allan had refused to respond to his letters and requests for money, but Poe didn't stop trying to gain his estranged foster father's help. After his harsh letter in January, Poe wrote Allan at least five more letters from February to December in 1831, begging for help in all of them.

In early 1831, Poe joined his widowed paternal aunt, Maria Clemm; his grandmother, Elizabeth Cairns Poe; his young cousins Virginia and Henry Clemm; and his brother, Henry, in their poverty-stricken home on Wilks Street. Maria Clemm would become an important figure in Poe's life, serving as his most stable mother figure and later his mother-in-law. He affectionately called her "Muddy." She helped support the family as a seamstress but was not beyond taking her young daughter, Virginia, out on the streets with a donation basket in times of desperation. Little Virginia took a strong liking to her older cousin, "Eddy," as she and her mother called him. Poe tutored her, and became quite fond of her too. The nature of their relationship will forever be speculated about and debated among scholars, but they would marry in either 1835 or 1836. (More later on the debate over when they officially married!)

Poe's brother, Henry, died on August 1, 1831, after a struggle with tuberculosis exacerbated by alcoholism. In 1833, the family moved into a tiny rowhouse on Amity Street where Poe's paralytic, bedridden grandmother would take her last breath two years later. The family relied heavily on her pension check, granted by the government for her husband's service in the American Revolution. When she died, the financial blow changed the family dynamic: By 1835, Henry Clemm had gone to sea, and he was never seen, heard, or spoken of again. It's believed that he died at sea. Maria and Virginia became Poe's family and support system.

THE MORE YOU KNOW

Apparently, after Poe's brother, Henry, died, Poe was arrested for debts his brother was responsible for. While there is no evidence that supports Poe's statement that he was arrested, both he and his aunt, Maria Clemm, wrote to John Allan, begging for money to settle the matter. This would be the first of many times Maria advocated for her nephew throughout their lives together. It is uncertain whether John Allan sent them anything.

Mary Starr & Poe's Favorite Song

During Poe's years in Baltimore, he fell in love with a seventeen-year-old girl named Mary Starr, who lived around the corner from Poe's house on Amity Street. Mary had long golden hair and a fair complexion that Poe was enamored of. Poe's cousin Virginia would assist in the romance between her cousin "Eddy" and his girlfriend by hand delivering love letters between the two.

Mary recalled, "[Poe] was handsome, but intellectually so, not a pretty man. He had the way and the power to draw any one to him. He was very fascinating, and any young girl would have fallen in love with him." When Mary sent Poe a lock of her golden hair as a token of her affection, things accelerated. Poe frequented her home, and it was at that point her family realized the two were romantically involved. They quickly moved to discourage the relationship. Mary's brother reminded her that Poe couldn't even support himself, let alone a wife. While there was no formal engagement between them, Poe proposed the idea and Mary kept an open mind about it.

Mary used to play piano and sing Poe's favorite song, "Come, Rest in This Bosom." One day, one of her brother's friends requested that she sing it for him in Poe's presence, knowing that it would likely get under Poe's skin. Pacing back and forth, biting his nails, Poe finally grabbed the sheet music from Mary and threw it to the floor. This was the first spectacle Poe made of himself in front of her family. The other, which caused their breakup, was after Poe had a few glasses of champagne with some West Point buddies who were visiting Baltimore. Poe showed up at Mary's house quite inebriated and attempted to chase her inside before he was intercepted by her mother. Poe claimed that Mary was his wife "in the sight of Heaven" and that he had a right to see her. Her mother insisted he go home to bed, and Mary subsequently ended the romance.

LITERARY CONNECTIONS

There is a lost poem by Poe to Mary Starr that he had published in a Baltimore paper and addressed "To Mary." The poem was incredibly harsh, with accusations of disloyalty and volatility. According to her nephew, all of Mary's friends and family knew it was about her, which embarrassed her. The poem caused only greater scorn among Mary's circle for the young poet.

Baltimore Saturday Visiter

On June 15, 1833, the *Baltimore Saturday Visiter* announced a contest that would award $50 for the best tale and $25 for the best poem. The judges were three of Baltimore's finest citizens: Dr. James Henry Miller, John H.B. Latrobe, and finally, John P. Kennedy, who would become one of Poe's greatest friends and supporters. With his family in desperate need of money, Poe entered this contest in the hope of winning some income for the household.

Poe submitted a number of works that were narrowed down to "The Coliseum" for the poetry category and "MS. Found in a Bottle" for the tale category. Out of one hundred entries, the judges short-listed both Poe's tale (which was unmatched by any other story submission) and his poem, along with another poem by a man named Henry Wilton titled "The Song of the Winds." Poe ultimately won the prize for best tale by a landslide, and Henry Wilton won the best poem. It turned out that Wilton was actually John Hewitt, the editor of the *Visiter.* When Poe found this out, he was livid.

Poe ran into Hewitt on the street and confronted him about his "underhanded means" of winning the poetry prize money that Poe deserved and needed desperately. According to Hewitt, Poe's eyes "flash[ed] with anger" as he verbally assaulted him. Tempers rose, and Hewitt delivered a fist directly to Poe's face that staggered him. Poe was a bit smaller than Hewitt, but according to those who knew him, he had a toughness that made it seem like it would be a fair fight. Before Poe was able to retaliate, though, friends intervened and separated the men.

LITERARY CONNECTIONS

After the *Baltimore Saturday Visiter* contest, Poe had a stronger taste for short story writing than he ever had before. He would tap into a whole new side of his creative genius with his pursuit of short story and genre writing. Baltimore has the distinction of giving birth not only to Poe as a short story writer but also to Poe as Master of the Macabre. Poe wrote and published his first short stories while living in Baltimore, as well as his first tales of horror (more on these later).

"Metzengerstein" & *"Berenice"*

Just one year before Poe won the *Baltimore Saturday Visiter* contest, he published a short story with a German title, "Metzengerstein," which is considered his first work of gothic fiction. The story was submitted to a contest as well, which was held by Philadelphia's *Saturday Courier*. Poe didn't win this contest, but his story was published in the *Courier* a week after the winning tale appeared. The *Courier* went on to publish more of Poe's works in the subsequent months.

Poe exaggerated the themes of gothic fiction in "Metzengerstein," which has scholars debating whether he meant the story to be taken seriously. Some suggest that it was supposed to be a satire of gothic fiction of the time. However, when Poe published his next horror tale, "Berenice," in 1835, there was no doubt among scholars that his intentions were to pen something truly gruesome and horrific. "Berenice" is arguably one of Poe's most violent tales, with a plot filled to the brim with obsession, premature burial, grave desecration, and body mutilation. These themes are also found in later works by Poe.

Egaeus, the narrator of "Berenice," is set to marry his cousin, Berenice, before her premature death puts a stop to the union. The tale likely had some biographical context, as Poe was growing closer to his cousin Virginia. There was talk of marriage between the two, which would be arranged the same year that "Berenice" was published. Maria Clemm encouraged the marriage. Poe wrote tenaciously in an attempt to support his little family and now his prospective wife, also publishing five other tales and four poems the same year. In Baltimore, Poe really started to see the attention that short stories could bring his career.

THE MORE YOU KNOW

When Poe published "Berenice" in the *Southern Literary Messenger* in 1835, he had to apologize to his editor for the story's "bad taste." However, Poe noted that despite the controversy "Berenice" caused, a writer had to be *read* to be appreciated. Poe proved that he knew his audience. He proved that the public outcry only meant that his work was being read, and therefore he was appreciated. Today, Poe's theory still rings true. Many are engrossed by all things weird and controversial, and Poe's writing continues to be beloved.

Opening Lines of "Berenice"

Misery is manifold. The wretchedness of earth is multiform. Overreaching the wide horizon like the rainbow, its hues are as various as the hues of that arch, as distinct too, yet as intimately blended. Overreaching the wide horizon like the rainbow! How is it that from Beauty I have derived a type of unloveliness?—from the covenant of Peace a simile of sorrow? But thus is it. And as, in ethics, Evil is a consequence of Good, so, in fact, out of Joy is sorrow born. Either the memory of past bliss is the anguish of to-day, or the agonies which *are*, have their origin in the ecstasies which *might have been*. I have a tale to tell in its own essence rife with horror—I would suppress it were it not a record more of feelings than of facts.

"A State of Starvation"

In 1833, Poe made his last written attempt to reach his foster father, John Allan: "It has now been more than two years since you have assisted me, and more than three since you have spoken to me. I feel little hope that you will pay any regard to this letter, but still I cannot refrain from making one more attempt to interest you in my behalf. . . .I am perishing—absolutely perishing for want of aid. And yet I am not idle—nor addicted to any vice—nor have I committed any offence against society which would render me deserving of so hard a fate. For God's sake pity me, and save me from destruction."

After not getting a reply, Poe paid him an unannounced visit in February 1834. Allan, now dying, had been confined to an armchair, since lying down on a bed caused him discomfort. As Allan's wife, Louisa, tended to him, she heard the front doorbell ring. When she opened the door, a young man stood there requesting to see Mr. Allan. Louisa, having never actually met Poe, was unaware who the young man was. She informed him that Allan's physicians prohibited any visitors besides nurses and attempted to close the door. Poe, quite familiar with the layout of the Allan mansion, pushed past Louisa and ran up to his dying foster father's bedroom.

When Poe entered Allan's room, Louisa not far behind him, Allan looked at Poe, raised his cane above his head, and threatened to strike Poe with it if he got within reach. He ordered his foster son out of the house, and Poe left the residence. Allan died the following month, on March 27, 1834. Poe lost the only father he ever truly had, as well as a potential source of money that was (rarely) accessible to him. The wealthy Allan left nothing in his will to Poe.

Poe strove even harder to make a steady income. He reached out to John P. Kennedy, one of the judges who awarded him the *Baltimore Saturday Visiter* prize, and asked for his help in securing a teaching position in Baltimore. When Kennedy finally saw Poe, he recalled that he was "in a state of starvation." He gave Poe all the assistance he could, including food, clothing, and a horse to use whenever he wanted. Kennedy said that this "brought [Poe] up from the very verge of despair." Kennedy then wrote to his friend Thomas Willis White, the owner of the *Southern Literary Messenger*, asking if he could offer Poe a permanent position at his magazine.

--------- THE MORE YOU KNOW ---------

At the beginning of their friendship, John P. Kennedy invited Poe to dinner, but Poe declined the invitation "for reasons of the most humiliating in nature [in] my personal appearance. You may conceive my deep mortification in making this disclosure to you—but it was necessary." This made Kennedy sympathetic to Poe even before meeting him in person.

Southern Literary Messenger

The *Southern Literary Messenger* was established in Richmond, Virginia, in 1834 by Thomas Willis White. It was considered one of the most important periodicals in the South at the time, and White employed Poe for the first time as a staff writer and editor for a magazine (with the help of mutual friend John P. Kennedy) in August 1835. But Poe's employment with the *Messenger* would be rocky.

Poe left his aunt, Maria Clemm, and cousin Virginia in Baltimore and settled in Richmond to start his magazine career. His writings and criticism proved successful, as the *Messenger* increased its circulation shortly after his employment. White quickly promoted Poe to assistant editor, and raised his salary. But despite all the popularity Poe brought to the magazine, White was forced to fire him after Poe repeatedly got so drunk that it interfered with his work. White stated that "Mr. Poe was a fine gentleman when he was sober. He was ever kind and courtly, and such times every one liked him. But when he was drinking he was about one of the most disagreeable men I have ever met."

White hired Poe back a month later, after warning him about the dangers of alcohol and the necessity of separating himself from the bottle to be successful. Poe's temperament, periods of unreliability, and controversial reviews would have been a lot for anyone to manage—not to mention he was smitten with White's daughter—and in December 1836, White removed Poe as assistant editor. He offered to keep him on as a staff writer; instead, Poe left the magazine altogether. While Poe worked at the *Southern Literary Messenger* for a little more than a year, he would contribute to the magazine until his death in 1849.

THE MORE YOU KNOW

The Poe Museum in Richmond, Virginia, owns the desk and chair where Poe worked during his employment at the *Southern Literary Messenger*. What's odd about the chair is that the back of it is missing, having been sawed off by Poe's boss. Purportedly, Thomas Willis White sawed off the back so that Poe wouldn't be too comfortable, prompting more productivity. Another speculation is that White wanted to see when Poe was slouching in his seat (a sign that he had been drinking).

Eliza White

For some time during Poe's employment with Thomas White's *Southern Literary Messenger*, he lived at his employer's home. It was there that he met fifteen-year-old Eliza, White's youngest daughter. According to schoolmates and other people who knew her, she was an intelligent young woman with "a slender [figure], graceful blonde [hair], and deep blue eyes." The relationship between her and Poe (if there ever truly was one) is rife with speculation, rumor, and unreliable accounts.

The story is that Poe fell in love with Eliza and they were engaged to be married. Eliza's father (Poe's boss) approved of a union between the two on the condition that Poe stay sober. But this is thought to be a rumor, considering that in September 1835, Poe had been issued a license in Baltimore to marry his cousin Virginia. It doesn't make sense that Poe would have been engaged to Eliza at the same time. However, some scholars believe that if Maria Clemm (Poe's aunt) had heard about a possible romance between Poe and another woman, it could have been the reason she pushed her young daughter into a hasty marriage with Poe.

The rumored relationship between Poe and Eliza supposedly ended after Poe proved he couldn't stay away from the bottle. They remained on good terms, though, and during

Virginia's later illness and death in 1847, Eliza visited Poe and his family at their cottage in Fordham, New York. She was also one of the few attendees at Poe and Virginia's wedding in 1836. In her later life, Maria Clemm addressed rumors about Eliza White and Poe, stating that Eliza was no more than a friend to him.

--- **LITERARY CONNECTIONS** ---

During the time he knew Eliza, Poe published a poem in the *Southern Literary Messenger* titled "Lines Written in an Album" and dedicated it to her. However, Poe had already written this poem in an album belonging to his cousin Eliza Herring. He even published it again years later, dedicating it to another woman, Frances Sargent Osgood, substituting "Fair maiden" for the name Eliza. It was the poem that kept on giving!

"Lines Written in an Album"

Eliza!—let thy generous heart
   From its present pathway part not!
Being every thing which now thou art,
   Be nothing which thou art not.
So with the world thy gentle ways—
   Thy unassuming beauty—
And truth shall be a theme of praise
   Forever—and love a duty.

The Tomahawk Man

Within the short time that Poe worked for the *Southern Literary Messenger*, he established himself as not only a poet, a short story writer, and an editor but also a scathing literary critic. His boss, Thomas White, had given him control of the book review section of the magazine, and Poe sought this opportunity to review a novel by a prominent New York journalist, Theodore Sedgwick Fay. The extremely harsh review kick-started Poe's career as one of the most fearsome literary critics of the nineteenth century.

Many magazines like the *Messenger* survived by making friends with other periodicals, often puffing each other up for the public. But Poe was known to loathe this practice, having a high standard for literature, which he wouldn't squander with fake-nice reviews. His criticism often included nitpicking grammatical errors and addressing illogical reasoning. He would also comment on technicalities of the writing, which he often deemed unsuccessful. Over the years, Poe challenged some of the most popular literary celebrities of his day.

On January 3, 1849, *Holden's Dollar Magazine* published a caricature of Poe as the "Tomahawk Man," illustrated by a friend of Poe's, the artist F.O.C. Darley. It was accompanied by these verses:

> With tomahawk upraised for deadly blow,
> Behold our literary Mohawk, Poe!
> Sworn tyrant he o'er all who sin in verse—
> His own the standard, damns he all that's worse;
> And surely not for this shall he be blamed—
> For worse than his deserves that it be damned!
>
> Augustine Joseph Hickey Duganne

Poe's harshly critical reviews were another reason why White ultimately demoted him from assistant editor. In a letter to author Nathaniel Beverley Tucker, White wrote that he was afraid Poe's reviews would tank the magazine: "Highly as I think of Mr. Poe's talents, I shall be forced to give him notice in a week or so at the farthest. . . .Added to all this, I am cramped by him in the exercise of my own judgement, as to what articles I shall or shall not admit into my work. It is true that I neither have his sagacity, nor his learning—but I do believe I know a handspike from a saw." Even after Poe left the *Messenger* and worked for other publications, throughout his career he never hesitated to wield his tomahawk.

LITERARY CONNECTIONS

Henry Wadsworth Longfellow was one of the most popular American poets of the nineteenth century. However, his status didn't stop Poe from attacking him with his critical pen. Poe claimed that Longfellow's fame was acquired unfairly and publicly called him out for plagiarism.

"My Love, My Own Sweetest Sissy, My Darling Little Wifey"

On August 29, 1835, Poe, "blinded with tears," wrote an emotional letter to his aunt, Maria Clemm. He had just moved out of the family home in Baltimore to work in Richmond after having lived with her and Virginia and helped support them. The letter from Maria that Poe was replying to has been lost, but based on Poe's reply, his cousin Neilson Poe was offering to take young Virginia under his roof to support her and give her a proper education. Maria wrote to Poe to tell him of these plans, and Poe responded with a letter expressing his "deepest anxiety."

The family had struggled from the start, but at this point, Maria had lost her mother (whose pension was paying the rent), her son was about to go off to sea, and Poe had left to start his magazine career in Richmond. Maria was struggling, with only her young daughter at her side. Some believe she appealed to Neilson to take Virginia in, while others theorize that she was using Virginia to manipulate Poe's emotions as a tactic to get him to take them both in.

Regardless of the context for Maria's letter, Poe pleaded with his aunt not to accept Neilson's offer, and he invited both her and Virginia to move into his house with him in

Richmond. He closed the letter with a message to Virginia, addressing her as "My love, my own sweetest Sissy, my darling little wifey" and asking her to "think well before you break the heart of your Cousin, Eddy." A marriage license was issued to Poe and Virginia a month later.

THE MORE YOU KNOW

Despite Poe's love for his cousin/wife, there are only two known letters from him to her. The first was his August 1835 letter to his aunt, where he addressed Virginia. The second was a short letter written to her in 1846. On the other hand, Poe wrote a substantial number of letters to his aunt while he was traveling, even while he was married to Virginia. Because of this, scholars believe that Poe considered Maria, not his wife, the head of the house while he was away.

Opening Lines of Poe's Letter to Maria Clemm and Virginia, August 29, 1835

My dearest Aunty,

I am blinded with tears while writing this letter—I have no wish to live another hour. Amid sorrow, and the deepest anxiety your letter reached—and you well know how little I am able to bear up under the pressure of grief. My bitterest enemy would pity me could he now read my heart. My last my last my only hold on life is cruelly torn away—I have no desire to live and *will not*. But let my duty be done. I love, *you know* I love Virginia passionately devotedly. I cannot express in words the fervent devotion I feel towards my dear little cousin—my own darling. (. . .) The tone of your letter wounds me to the soul—Oh Aunty, aunty you loved me once—how can you be so cruel now? You speak of Virginia acquiring accomplishments, and entering into society—you speak in so *worldly* a tone. Are you sure she would be more happy. Do you think any one could love her more dearly than I? She will have far—very far better opportunities of entering into society here than with N. P. Every one here receives me with open arms. Adieu my dear aunty. I *cannot advise you*. Ask Virginia. Leave it to her. Let me have, under her own hand, a letter, bidding me *good bye*—forever—and I may die—my heart will break—but I will say no more.

A Secret Wedding and a Thirteen-Year-Old Bride

On September 22, 1835, twenty-six-year-old Edgar Allan Poe and his thirteen-year-old cousin, Virginia Eliza Clemm, were issued a marriage license in Baltimore. Based on the letters sent between them at the time, Poe's aunt (Virginia's mother), Maria Clemm, fully supported this union. In fact, there is speculation that the marriage was practically arranged by Maria, who was afraid of losing her nephew's support of the household after he had moved to Richmond to work at the *Southern Literary Messenger*. There is also debate about whether a "secret" ceremony took place at this time; regardless, a public wedding happened eight months later, on May 16, 1836.

The official ceremony was held in the boardinghouse where Poe, Virginia, and Maria were staying in Richmond. Poe's boss, Thomas White, and his daughter, Eliza, were among the few in attendance. A Presbyterian minister named Amasa Converse married the couple. Whether Converse knew her real age or not, young Virginia was listed on the marriage bond as being twenty-one years old.

Poe and Virginia never had any children, and Poe referred to Virginia interchangeably as "Sissy," "Wifey," and "cousin" throughout their marriage. Some scholars believe that Poe waited until she was at least sixteen before consummating the marriage, if they even consummated it at all.

Following the ceremony was a delicious meal with a wedding cake prepared by Maria and the owner of the boardinghouse, Mrs. James Yarrington. Poe and his child bride honeymooned in Petersburg, Virginia, the next day, at the coffeehouse and hotel owned by poet and magazine editor Hiram Haines. In 1840, Haines offered Virginia a pet fawn as a late wedding gift. Unable to transport the baby deer to Philadelphia, where the family was living at the time, Poe declined the gift, writing to Haines, "[Virginia] desires me to thank you with all her heart—but, unhappily, I cannot point out a mode of conveyance. What can be done? Perhaps some opportunity may offer itself hereafter—some friend from Petersburg may be about to pay us a visit. In the meantime accept our best acknowledgments, precisely as if the little fellow were already nibbling the grass before our windows in Philadelphia."

Opening Lines of "Morella"

With a feeling of deep yet most singular affection I
regarded my friend Morella. Thrown by accident into
her society many years ago, my soul, from our first
meeting, burned with fires it had never before known;
but the fires were not of Eros, and bitter and tor-
menting to my spirit was the gradual conviction that
I could in no manner define their unusual meaning, or
regulate their vague intensity. Yet we met; and fate
bound us together at the altar; and I never spoke
of passion, nor thought of love. She, however, shunned
society, and, attaching herself to me alone, rendered me
happy. It is a happiness to wonder;—it is a happiness
to dream.

"Maelzel's Chess Player"

With a wife and mother-in-law to support, Poe continued to write. In April 1836, he published an essay in the *Southern Literary Messenger* that attempted to explain the workings of a robotic chess player that had recently made its debut in America. The automaton was devised in the 1770s by a Hungarian inventor named Wolfgang von Kempelen. Audiences would watch as the robot, outfitted in a robe and turban and known as The Mechanical Turk, or simply The Turk, while seated at a chessboard on top of a large wooden box beat any opponent that challenged it to a game—even winning against Benjamin Franklin, then serving as US ambassador to France. When Napoleon challenged The Mechanical Turk, he attempted to cheat, causing the automaton to swipe all the pieces off the board.

When The Mechanical Turk was sold to a man named Johann Nepomuk Maelzel, he took it to America, where newspapers across the country headlined this amazing piece of technology. Crowds were perplexed by this machine that was unlike anything they had ever seen. Maelzel would open the different compartments of the automaton to show the audience the gears and mechanics inside and to prove there were no tricks involved and no human was operating the machine. When Poe caught wind of this sensation, he made it his mission to debunk the workings of the chess-playing automaton. He knew that it had to be some sort of hoax.

Poe's lengthy essay, titled "Maelzel's Chess Player," delved deep into every facet of The Turk. His conclusion was that a small man had to be operating the automaton while hiding inside the wooden cabinet, invisible to the audience due to an illusion created by sliding panels and mirrors when Maelzel opened the cabinet. Poe was applauded across the nation for solving this great mystery, and his essay was called "ingenious." While Maelzel's chess-playing Turk was a sensation across Europe and America, it also became known as the puzzle that inspired Poe to create some of his most sensationalistic stories and even an entire genre.

LITERARY CONNECTIONS

The deduction and ratiocination Poe used to decode The Mechanical Turk was a system he would use for his fictional detective, C. Auguste Dupin, in the first ever detective story, published five years later. After Poe's debunking of The Turk, he went on to create his own hoaxes, duping audiences and advancing sensationalism.

Philadelphia

After leaving his first job at the *Southern Literary Messenger*, Poe moved his family out of Richmond to find work elsewhere. They settled briefly in New York before making their way to Philadelphia, yet another major publishing capital in America. From 1838 until 1844, the city, which had a lot to offer Poe professionally, offered the family stability. Here, Poe was unquestionably the most productive he would ever be in his career.

The family first settled in a boardinghouse and would live in three additional places throughout their six years in Philadelphia. One residence was on the outskirts of town, and the Poe family would continue to live in quiet spots in other cities they moved to, away from the bustle of the city's center.

Poe was able to excel in his career while he wrote and published a variety of works in Philadelphia, but this success didn't bring in much money. While the city's dozens of daily and weekly newspapers gave Poe plenty of outlets for his work, they offered meager pay for submitted material. Poe tried to make a living solely off his writing, but the little money he earned from it meant he struggled financially and the family remained impoverished (nothing they weren't used to).

During this time, Poe had been working on the only novel he would write in his entire career, and it was published not long after the move to Philadelphia. (More on this novel later.) He also published his first book of short stories, along with a book on seashells. His most successful story, "The Gold-Bug," was published here, and he furthered his career as an editor, working for two different publications.

Sadly, Poe was continuing his self-destruction at every turn, dependent on the escape that alcohol provided him. In a letter written to a friend in April 1841, he tried to explain his relationship with alcohol: "In short, it sometimes happened that I was completely intoxicated. For some days after each excess I was invariably confined to bed. But it is now quite four years since I have abandoned every kind of alcoholic drink—four years, with the exception of a single deviation . . . when I was induced to resort to the occasional use of *cider*, with the hope of relieving a nervous attack." Poe would go months or even years without drinking. However, when he did drink, it ravaged his life.

LITERARY CONNECTIONS

Poe's other well-known tales published in Philadelphia include "The Fall of the House of Usher," "The Murders in the Rue Morgue," "The Masque of the Red Death," "The Pit and the Pendulum," "The Tell-Tale Heart," and "The Black Cat."

The Narrative of Arthur Gordon Pym of Nantucket

Within his first few months in Philadelphia, Poe published his only novel, *The Narrative of Arthur Gordon Pym of Nantucket*, which featured an unusually long subtitle of over one hundred words. On the book's title page, Poe used the text of the title and subtitle to suggest the shape of a ship.

The novel is about a sea voyage gone wild, featuring the shipwrecked crew of the *Grampus*. To survive, the crew draws straws to determine who will be sacrificed to provide meat for everyone else. (This was actually morally acceptable according to a code among sailors.) In Poe's story, the short straw is drawn by a young cabin boy named Richard Parker, who is promptly stabbed to death and consumed, enabling the crew to survive until they are rescued.

Poe purposely published the novel without making it obvious that it was a piece of fiction, something he often did with his writing to hoax his readers. Poe's details about oceanic navigation, for example, were so accurate that it was easy to pass off the novel as truth. *Pym* received decent reviews, but writing a whole novel was tedious work. That wasn't the only reason Poe primarily stuck to short stories and poems. Poe believed that a piece of writing should be read from start to finish in one sitting to maintain "the unity of effect." (The "effect" is whatever the author's sole reason for writing the work is.) According to Poe, if a reader had to put a piece of writing down before finishing it, its intended effect would be lost.

Despite the novel's lack of popularity at the time, it inspired the French author Jules Verne's two-volume novel, *An Antarctic Mystery*, published in 1897. The novel is fan fiction serving as a sequel to *Pym*.

────────── **LITERARY CONNECTIONS** ──────────

In 1884, a yacht named the *Mignonette* left England for Australia but was sunk by a storm, leaving the four-member crew stranded in a lifeboat with insufficient provisions. Just like their counterparts in Poe's novel *The Narrative of Arthur Gordon Pym of Nantucket*, the crew needed to survive long enough to be rescued. They too decided to draw straws to select who would be sacrificed for the survival of the others. The crew member that drew the short straw was a seventeen-year-old cabin boy whose name, like the character's in *Pym*, was Richard Parker.

Poe the Conchologist?

While living in Philadelphia, Poe wrote his bestselling book in his lifetime. Many readers have probably never even heard of it, never mind read it: a textbook on seashells titled *The Conchologist's First Book*, published in April 1839. While Poe did have a passion for science, this biology book was not driven by Poe's love of seashells. The reason Poe wrote the book was because of a man named Thomas Wyatt, who was a conchologist.

Wyatt used to travel the country in the late 1830s to early 1840s giving lectures about seashells. At the end of his lectures, he would try to sell his book, *A Manual of Conchology* (published in 1838), to audience members. The problem was, his book was a bit pricey at $8 (over $250 today!), so, not many would end up buying it. Wyatt wanted to condense the information into a book he could sell at a cheaper price. However, when he went to his publishers with this prospect, they refused to publish a book that would undersell the one already in circulation. That is where Poe came in. Wyatt contracted Poe for $50 to write a new book and have it published under his name. With Poe's name on the book (in addition to its cheaper price tag) Wyatt would have no problem selling it on his lecture tour.

Poe's book on seashells proved to be such a hit that a second edition was published just the next year. A third edition followed in 1845. The success of *The Conchologist's First Book* led to a publisher agreeing to publish Poe's first book of short stories, *Tales of the Grotesque and Arabesque*. Poe also had some pull now as a bestselling author when he applied to editorial jobs, and he landed a position at *Burton's Gentleman's Magazine* in May 1839.

THE MORE YOU KNOW

As Poe was reworking Thomas Wyatt's book on conchology, he noticed something about the engravings of the seashells that seemed wrong to him. The engravings were organized by most to least complex, and Poe thought that they should be arranged the opposite way. And he was right. Charles Darwin's theory of evolution in *On the Origin of Species,* published twenty years later in 1859, solidified Poe's idea that seashells started off less complex and evolved into more complex species over time. Poe came up with this idea on his own, before scientists could validate his thinking with research and evidence! Today, biology textbooks arrange organisms from least to most complex, just like Poe did in *The Conchologist's First Book.*

Burton's Gentleman's Magazine & Penn Magazine

The June 1839 issue of *Burton's Gentleman's Magazine* announced that Edgar Allan Poe had been given an editorial role at the magazine. This came after about a year of Poe earning a small income from freelance work while living in Philadelphia. *Burton's Gentleman's Magazine* was founded in 1837 by William Evans Burton, an actor and comedian from England. Although Burton had reviewed Poe's literary work poorly, Poe still approached him about employing him as assistant editor. The most popular work that Poe published in Burton's magazine was "The Fall of the House of Usher," which appeared in the September 1839 issue.

Since Burton was often engaged in theatrical endeavors, he wasn't often around to help Poe with the magazine, and Poe had to take on managerial duties despite being only an assistant editor. It's no surprise then that Poe was very angry when Burton wrote to him to tell him he would be cutting his pay. Poe replied: "When you address me again preserve if you can, the dignity of a gentleman. If by accident you have taken it into your head *by any sad accident* that I am to be insulted with impunity I can only assume that you are an ass. . . .Upon the whole I am not willing to admit that you have greatly overpaid me. That I did not do 4 times as much as I did for the Magazine, was your own fault. At first I wrote long articles which you deemed inadmissable, & never did I suggest any to *you* which you had not some immediate and decided objection. Of course I grew discouraged & could feel no interest in the Journal."

Unbeknown to Poe, Burton was slowly undermining his literary prospects. Burton had plans to open a national theater in Philadelphia and was secretly attempting to sell his magazine. He ultimately sold it to George Rex Graham, publisher of *Atkinson's Casket*, for $1 per subscriber (which amounted to $3,500). Graham combined the two publications to form *Graham's Magazine*, where Poe would also find employment. When Poe left *Burton's Gentleman's Magazine*, he had already announced plans to start a publication of his own called *Penn Magazine*. Poe wanted to be free from the control of somebody else and have complete liberty in editing and publishing a magazine. But he had to continue working for others while he gained the subscribers and funding to establish his *Penn Magazine*.

THE MORE YOU KNOW

Poe published his prospectus for his *Penn Magazine* in Philadelphia's *Saturday Evening Post* on June 6, 1840. This magazine, which would be under his complete control, would be published in Philadelphia on the first of the month. However, illness and financial problems plagued him, and sadly, the magazine never came to fruition.

Tales of the Grotesque and Arabesque

Poe's first collection of short stories, titled *Tales of the Grotesque and Arabesque*, appeared in 1840 after Poe had to convince the publishers (Lea and Blanchard) that the two-volume set would be worth printing. Unfortunately, Poe was overly optimistic about the success of this edition. It included some of his well-known stories along with lesser-known ones. "Morella," "William Wilson," "The Fall of the House of Usher," "Ligeia," and "Berenice" were among the hits.

Even with Poe's success as a poet, a literary critic, a textbook author, an editor, and an award-winning short story writer, the publishers were apprehensive about printing this edition of his short stories, suspecting that it wouldn't sell. They wrote to Poe, promising to print 1,750 copies at their own risk, keeping the potentially small profit for themselves if those copies sold. They also promised to give Poe a few copies for his own distribution and the ownership of the book's copyright (which didn't help him much financially). Poe accepted the offer.

The country was already facing financial difficulties at the time, and *Tales of the Grotesque and Arabesque* didn't sell well at all. Poe wrote to the publishers, offering to sell them the copyright, and their reply pretty much summed up the circumstances: "The copyright of the Tales would be of no value to us; when we undertook their publication, it was solely to oblige you and not with any view to profit, and on this ground it was urged by you. We should not therefore be now called upon or expected to purchase the copyright when we have no expectation of realizing the Capital placed in the volumes." Less than a year later, Poe wrote to the publishers again with the hope of publishing another volume, which would be full of all-new tales. They declined his offer.

LITERARY CONNECTIONS

Tales of the Grotesque and Arabesque was not Poe's first attempt at publishing a collection of short stories. Five years earlier, he had attempted to find a publisher for a group of stories that he titled *Tales of the Folio Club*, written around a group of characters who called themselves the Folio Club. Although this collection never came to be, the stories were all published between 1832 and 1836 in the *Philadelphia Saturday Courier* and the *Southern Literary Messenger*. Many of the tales also appeared in *Tales of the Grotesque and Arabesque*.

Graham's Magazine

A financial crisis suspended banks all over the United States in February 1841. Money was extremely difficult to obtain, and this caused Poe to postpone his *Penn Magazine*. However, by the end of the month, he had secured an editorial position at *Graham's Magazine*, which had recently launched. Yet again, Poe was working as an editor of someone else's publication instead of having full control and ownership of his own. But he would be getting a salary to help support his wife and mother-in-law.

Graham's became known for its art and fashion plates, which Poe loathed. He thought that too much of the magazine was composed of "contemptable" art and of love tales. *Graham's* was also where Poe met the man who would become his colleague, friend, rival, literary executor, and infamous defamer: Rufus Wilmot Griswold. Griswold would go down in history as the villain of Poe's biography. When Poe left the magazine in 1842, Griswold had taken his place as editor and was even paid a slightly higher salary.

THE MORE YOU KNOW

Apparently, readers were not too happy about Rufus Wilmot Griswold's replacing Poe at *Graham's*. On June 23, 1842, Jesse E. Dow of the Washington *Index* commented, "We would give more for Edgar A. Poe's toe nail, than we would for Rueful Grizzle's soul, unless we wanted a milk-strainer. Them's our sentiments."

Like many of the positions Poe held at magazines, his time with *Graham's* was short. He left the magazine after only a year of employment there. Poe persisted in his quest to get his own magazine off the ground. In fact, when he had the opportunity to meet Robert Tyler (son of the sitting president, John Tyler) in March 1843, he attempted to solicit a subscription to his magazine from Tyler, who in turn offered him a government job. When Poe was supposed to interview for the job, he instead disappeared for a few days, later claiming that he was ill. It's believed that Poe was recovering from a drinking binge. Whatever the reason for missing the interview, he destroyed his chance at securing the government position that would have granted him a yearly salary of $1,500 (nearly twice the amount he was making at *Graham's*).

The Red Death

The year 1842 marked the beginning of the end for Poe's beloved wife, Virginia. At nineteen years old, she exhibited the first signs of consumption, a disease Poe knew all too well. In a letter to a friend dated February 3, 1842, Poe wrote, "My dear little wife has been dangerously ill. About a fortnight since, in singing, she ruptured a blood-vessel, and it was only on yesterday that the physicians gave me any hope of her recovery. You might imagine the agony I have suffered, for you know how devotedly I love her. But to-day the prospect brightens, and I trust that this bitter cup of misery will not be my portion."

According to those who knew her, Virginia was a captivating vocalist, often playing the piano or harp to accompany her lovely singing voice. And despite the poverty that Poe and his family endured, he always afforded certain luxuries to his wife. Music was a passion of hers, and he provided her with musical instruments and lessons to pursue this passion. One day in 1842, while she was performing for her husband and mother, a coughing fit interrupted her. Splatters of blood collected on the handkerchief she held to her mouth. In subsequent accounts of Virginia's illness, Poe maintained that she ruptured a blood vessel while singing. But this was more than a ruptured blood vessel: It was the first sign of the disease that had taken his mother and brother. Consumption would eventually take his wife too, in just five years' time. Coincidentally, not only did all three people in Poe's life die of the same illness, but at the same age of twenty-four.

LITERARY CONNECTIONS

It's believed that Poe's "The Masque of the Red Death" was written as an allegory of consumption, the disease that his wife first exhibited signs of just months before he published the story. It was the leading cause of death in the United States until the turn of the twentieth century. Victims would experience incessant coughing fits, chest pain, fatigue, night sweats, and weight loss, and they would essentially waste away until their death.

Opening Lines of "The Masque of the Red Death"

The "Red Death" had long devastated the country. No pestilence had ever been so fatal, or so hideous. Blood was its Avatar and its seal—the redness and the horror of blood. There were sharp pains, and sudden dizziness, and then profuse bleeding at the pores, with dissolution. The scarlet stains upon the body and especially upon the face of the victim, were the pest ban which shut him out from the aid and from the sympathy of his fellowmen. And the whole seizure, progress and termination of the disease, were the incidents of half an hour. (...) And now was acknowledged the presence of the Red Death. He had come like a thief in the night. And one by one dropped the revellers in the blood-bedewed halls of their revel, and died each in the despairing posture of his fall. And the life of the ebony clock went out with that of the last of the gay. And the flames of the tripods expired. And Darkness and Decay and the Red Death held illimitable dominion over all.

Poe Meets Dickens

Over in England, a young Charles Dickens was making his debut as a successful author with his first novel, *The Pickwick Papers*, which was published in installments from 1836 to 1837. The novel shared themes with Poe's works: a beautiful woman, death, and madness. Poe praised Dickens's work in the *Southern Literary Messenger* in June 1836. In 1841, Poe read Dickens's fifth novel, *Barnaby Rudge*, which featured a talking raven. Poe would publish one of his best-known poems, "The Raven," four years later in 1845, which also featured a talking raven. Poe was a huge fan of Dickens's work, giving him more praise than any other writer of his time (except maybe Nathaniel Hawthorne).

In March 1842, Dickens visited Philadelphia during his tour of America to help advocate for a revised American copyright law. At the time, both American and English copyright laws aimed to safeguard the author's control of their writings and publications. However, the duration of the copyright protection and the ease of enforcing infringement claims were much more favorable in England than America. Also, due to the lack of international copyright, publishers in America could print and sell Dickens's work for free, which made it extremely competitive for American writers to sell their work. When Poe found out that Dickens would be visiting his city, he requested a meeting. They met at the United States Hotel, where Dickens was staying in Philadelphia.

The two writers discussed literature and compared the laws around publishing in each other's countries. Before they parted ways, Poe appealed to Dickens to get his *Tales of the Grotesque and Arabesque* published in England. Dickens agreed to make an effort to help but was unsuccessful. He later wrote to Poe, "I have mentioned it to publishers with whom I have influence, but they have, one and all, declined the venture." Dickens continued, "Do not for a moment suppose that I have ever thought of you but with a pleasant recollection; and that I am not at all times prepared to forward your views in this country." Poe's appreciation for Dickens fizzled after this. Dickens, however, remained a devoted admirer of Poe and even gave a substantial amount of money to Poe's impoverished aunt Maria Clemm nearly twenty years after Poe's death.

LITERARY CONNECTIONS

It's thought that *Barnaby Rudge* partly inspired Poe's "The Raven." At the end of Chapter 5 of *Barnaby Rudge*, the characters hear a tapping at the door and think it is coming from the shutter. This is similar to the opening stanzas of "The Raven," where the narrator hears a tapping that he thinks is at his door, but is actually at his "window lattice." Dickens even had a pet raven named Grip, which he had stuffed after it died. The taxidermy Grip is now on display at the Free Library of Philadelphia.

Poe Files for Bankruptcy

Edgar Allan Poe appreciated Dickens's mission to convince America to enact a copyright law, as this would have allowed Poe to make a little more money off his works. Poe lived his whole adult life in poverty. In fact, he and his family lived off nothing but bread and molasses for weeks in 1838. Poe relied on his writing for a meager income, but he relied more on the generosity of friends and creditors.

The Bankruptcy Act of 1841, passed by the US Congress (and repealed in 1843) allowed voluntary (or involuntary) debt relief for citizens. This came as a response to the Panic of 1837 and the six-year depression that followed. Poe unhesitatingly took advantage of this government assistance, filing for bankruptcy on December 19, 1842, while living in Philadelphia. In his petition, Poe listed himself as a "late editor," having left his position at *Graham's Magazine* earlier that year. Poe claimed that he owned no real property, his only possessions being the clothes on his back and some printed sheets (newspapers, magazines, and any material from a printing press). Most of the debts listed on the petition were for rent, personal loans from acquaintances, book dealers, music lessons for his wife, and medical debt.

The debts themselves ranged in amount from $4 to over $150. Poe's total debt was just over $2,000—about $80,000 today. Poe was among over 40,000 Americans who filed for bankruptcy under this act, and he was not the only well-known historical figure to do so. Abraham Lincoln and Mark Twain were two other nineteenth-century figures who had to file for bankruptcy in their lifetime. For the next seven years of Poe's life, he would never get ahead financially.

THE MORE YOU KNOW

Edgar Allan Poe's poverty and financial straits were never a secret to those who knew him. Poe's poverty has overshadowed other parts of his biography since the first writings about him. But it wasn't until around 2001 that it became known Poe had filed for bankruptcy, after an archivist came across Poe's file in the National Archives at Philadelphia.

Rufus Griswold's The Poets and Poetry of America

Perhaps the most important man in literature in the nineteenth century was Rufus Wilmot Griswold, a poet, critic, editor, and anthologist. His anthology *The Poets and Poetry of America* was first published in 1842 and became a major success. It saw several editions until 1877. When Poe caught wind of this prospective anthology by the man who had taken his place at *Graham's Magazine*, he reached out to Griswold in the hope that they could meet. The two had an agreeable meeting where they discussed Griswold's book, which was being prepared for press. During their conversation, Poe convinced Griswold to include him in the anthology. Poe sent him some poems for consideration.

When *The Poets and Poetry of America* was finally published on April 18, 1842, Poe was less than happy. Griswold had published three of Poe's poems but included them toward the back of the book. Poe called it an "outrageous humbug" and thought that the anthology focused too much on poets who didn't deserve the recognition while discounting many who did (like himself). When Griswold paid Poe to write a review of the anthology, Poe took the opportunity to get his frustrations out. While he did give the anthology a relatively favorable review, Poe made sure to object to many of the poets that Griswold chose to feature.

The two would fluctuate between friendship and enmity, exchanging praise and criticism of each other through the following years. Griswold would ultimately have the final word when he wrote a harsh obituary of Poe published a few days after his death (more on this later). Griswold quickly became the most infamous person in Poe's biography and the reason why so much information about Poe's personal character is skewed today.

LITERARY CONNECTIONS

Rufus Wilmot Griswold began a new anthology in 1845 titled *The Prose Writers of America*. As a critic, he knew that he couldn't leave Poe out of the edition over a trivial personal quarrel, so he wrote to him asking for a few submissions, stating, "Although I have some cause of personal quarrel with you, which you will easily enough remember, I do not under any circumstances permit, as you have repeatedly charged, my private griefs to influence my judgment as a critic, or its expressions. I retain, therefore, the early formed and well founded favorable opinions of your works." Poe was glad to have received this letter from Griswold and took responsibility for the strain in their friendship. In his reply, Poe wrote: "Dear Griswold—if you will permit me to call you so—Your letter occasioned me first pain and then pleasure:—pain because it gave me to see that I had lost, through my own folly, an honorable friend:—pleasure, because I saw in it a hope of reconciliation."

Poe's Autobiography

When Poe had to write a short autobiography for his section in Griswold's *The Poets and Poetry of America*, he treated it almost like a work of fiction. Poe knew that he had to have a fascinating narrative of his life to hook readers, so a little fabrication was in order. Poe condensed his whole life story onto a single sheet of paper, but what he wrote could hardly be classified as biographical. Poe lied multiple times throughout the piece, starting with his age.

Along with saying he was two years younger than he really was, Poe said that he came from one of the oldest and most respected families in Baltimore. This was only partly true: Poe's grandparents were respected, but they were not originally from Baltimore, having immigrated from Ireland in the mid-eighteenth century. Poe also claimed that he had been a soldier in Europe fighting for the Greek War of Independence. In writing these fantastical accounts of his life, Poe was creating a narrative that mirrored the life of his hero, Lord Byron.

Poe even smoothed out details about his time at the University of Virginia and West Point, casting himself in a more respectable light. His "autobiography" was printed nearly word for word in Griswold's anthology. After Poe's death, Griswold wrote a memoir of Poe for his four-volume edition of Poe's works. He pulled a lot of Poe's "facts" from this autobiography but added many of his own lies, along with slanders. This created a double layer of misinformation that subsequent biographers have had to sort through. For nearly two centuries, countless people have written about the life of Edgar Allan Poe, and his less-than-truthful autobiography didn't help early biographers get the facts straight. It is no wonder why the truth about Poe's life is still so elusive today!

—————— LITERARY CONNECTIONS ——————

While Poe's fabricated autobiography is the only autobiography of his that exists, there is reason to believe that some of his tales featured autobiographical elements. For example, "Eleonora," published in 1842, features a narrator who is in love with his cousin. In the story, the couple live with her mother, the narrator's aunt. This directly reflects Poe's life with his cousin/wife and aunt/mother-in-law.

Opening Lines of "Eleonora"

I am come of a race noted for vigor of fancy and ardor of passion. Men have called me mad; but the question is not yet settled, whether madness is or is not the loftiest intelligence—whether much that is glorious—whether all that is profound—does not spring from disease of thought—from moods of mind exalted at the expense of the general intellect. They who dream by day are cognizant of many things which escape those who dream only by night.

"The Philosophy of Furniture"

One thing that Poe left out of his autobiography was his love for interior decorating. Or perhaps his essay "The Philosophy of Furniture" could be considered more of a satirical work, given its humorous tone. It was published in *Burton's Gentleman's Magazine* in May 1840. While some dismiss this work as frivolous, others believe it may hide some very important messages. Poe was not known to write something for little-to-no reason. If it was written and published by Poe, it usually meant *something*.

In the essay, Poe describes his ideal room, which is approximately 30 feet long by 25 feet wide. A single door should be opposite two large windows with rosewood frames that open onto a veranda. An Argand lamp should provide light, since he believed that gas lighting was too harsh on the eyes. The color scheme (which dictates the character of the room) should be composed chiefly of silver and crimson, and featured in the silk curtains, carpet (which Poe describes as "the soul of the apartment"), sofas, and chairs. The curtains should be thick, and tied open with gold-colored rope. The wallpaper should have arabesque designs, while the walls should feature large landscape paintings and portraits of ethereal women.

Poe was not a fan of mirrors (he didn't often like how he looked), so no more than one circular mirror should be in the room, hung in such a way that no one could see their reflection from the sitting areas. The only large pieces included in the sitting areas should be two large sofas with matching chairs, a rosewood piano (to match the window frames), and an octagonal marble table. And of course no room of Edgar Allan Poe's would be complete without "two or three hundred magnificently bound books."

THE MORE YOU KNOW

Poe's essay "The Philosophy of Furniture" is thought to be an allegory for Americans' materialistic nature and society's obsession with wealth. Poe goes as far as saying, "As we grow rich, our ideas grow rusty." Poe believed that people were so dependent on material things as a reflection of their spiritual worth that it was harmful to their actual value as human beings.

Inventor of Detective Fiction

The mystery genre was certainly not a new thing when Edgar Allan Poe published "The Murders in the Rue Morgue" in 1841. However, with the publication of this story, he invented a new facet of the genre, one known today as detective fiction. The first thing he published as editor of *Graham's Magazine*, the story features a French detective named C. Auguste Dupin. The unnamed narrator, a friend of Dupin's, walks readers through the detective's solution to a gruesome double murder in the Rue Morgue.

"The Murders in the Rue Morgue" ends with a twist that many readers don't expect. (If you haven't read it yet and don't want spoilers, skip to the next paragraph!) The conclusion Dupin comes to is that the murderer was no human being but an orangutan, which belonged to a sailor. Two years prior to the story's publication, a live chimpanzee was exhibited at the Masonic Hall in Philadelphia. It's believed that Poe went to see this animal and was inspired by its very humanlike characteristics. When he invented the detective fiction story, the ape was on his mind.

Poe called "The Murders in the Rue Morgue" a "tale of ratiocination," which essentially means a tale of logical reasoning. This tale would be the first in a series by Poe that features his French detective, Dupin. The other tales are "The

Mystery of Marie Rogêt" and "The Purloined Letter." Dupin is the only recurring character in stories written by Poe. The three tales created the template for plots widely used in detective stories: a crime being solved after it happened, a crime being solved as it is happening, and a crime being solved that happened somewhere far away.

LITERARY CONNECTIONS

Sir Arthur Conan Doyle was the creator of the most famous detective in literature, Sherlock Holmes, who first appeared in print in 1887. But Doyle credited Poe with inspiring his detective series, going as far as saying, "Where was the detective story until Poe breathed the breath of life into it?" While Sherlock Holmes has been generations of readers' iconic detective, without Poe's Dupin, there would be no Holmes.

Opening Lines of "The Murders in the Rue Morgue"

It is not improbable that a few farther steps in phrenological science will lead to a belief in the existence, if not to the actual discovery and location of an organ of *analysis*. If this power (which may be described, although not defined, as the capacity for resolving thought into its elements) be not, in fact, an essential portion of what late philosophers term ideality, then there are indeed many good reasons for supposing it a primitive faculty. That it may be a constituent of ideality is here suggested in opposition to the vulgar dictum (founded, however, upon the assumptions of grave authority,) that the calculating and discriminating powers (causality and comparison) are at variance with the imaginative—that the three, in short, can hardly coexist. But, although thus opposed to received opinion, the idea will not appear ill-founded when we observe that the processes of invention or creation are strictly akin with the processes of resolution—the former being nearly, if not absolutely, the latter conversed.

Cryptography

When he was editor of *Graham's Magazine*, Poe became fascinated with cryptography, which coincided with his love for ratiocination. Cryptography is the practice of encoding and decoding hidden messages in language. Edgar Allan Poe was already encoding names in his poetry when in July 1841, he published an article, "A Few Words on Secret Writing," where he explains a bit about the history of cryptography and how to create and solve ciphers.

Not only did Poe enjoy creating his own ciphers, but he liked to solve them too. He even invited readers to submit their own ciphers to *Graham's* for him to solve, promising a free subscription to the magazine for whoever could create a cipher he couldn't solve. He solved nearly one hundred different submissions, one of them a nonsensical cipher that he proved was just a jumble of letters to throw him off. Nobody could stump Poe with a cryptograph, and nobody received a free subscription to *Graham's*.

But Poe was becoming overwhelmed with the number of entries he was getting, which left him little time to work on his poetry and prose. So, he turned the tables on his readers and offered two ciphers for *them* to solve. The shorter of the two looked like this:

```
, † § : ‡] [ ,? ‡ ) , [ ¡ ¶ ? , † , ) ¡ , § [ ¶ Þ , [ ,: ¶! [ . § ( , † § ¡
|| (? ⊥ ? , ** ( ⊥ ⊥ ¡ ( [ , ¶ * . ⊥ [ § ¶ § ¡ . ¶ ] ¿ , † § [ ? ( § [ : :
( † [ . ⊥ ( * ; ( || ( , † § ¡ ‡ [ * : , [! ¶ † || ] ? * ! ¶ ⊥ † § ¶ || ,
. ( ⊥ ¡ ( , ? ‡ § ( ¡☜ ¡ ¶ [ ¡ ¶ [ ? ( , ; § ‡ ☞ ‡ ] † § §: ( † [ †
[ ¶ ? ‡]: * ¡ ¶: ( § ? ] ! ! ¶ † § ‡ ] ; § ? ‡ † ¡ ‡ ⊥ ¶! ( , † §?
( || * ] [ § ¡ ' ! , : , , † § ☜ ) , ? || ¶ ? , § § (! ⊥ ¡ ( , † § † [ ‡
? ) * ] [ ⊥ : ? ] ||
```

The longer cipher was made up of a mix of Roman capital letters, lowercase letters, small capital letters, and inversions of these characters. Both of Poe's cryptographic messages went unsolved for over 150 years. The shorter one was finally solved by a man named Terence Whalen in 1991. This cipher turned out to be quoted lines from the final act of Joseph Addison's play, "Cato." In 2000, the longer cipher was solved by a software engineer named Gil Broza. This longer message turned out to be a play-on-words involving "sun," "son," "air," and "heir." Poe popularized cryptography in the nineteenth century and would use it in his story "The Gold-Bug."

─────────── THE MORE YOU KNOW ───────────

Before Poe published "A Few Words on Secret Writing" in *Graham's Magazine*, he claimed to have solved multiple cryptograms in a Philadelphia newspaper called *Alexander's Weekly Messenger*. Scholars have yet to find evidence of any cryptograms submitted or solved by Poe. Many think this was a tactic on Poe's part to puff himself up in order to gain readers' interest in cryptography.

"The Gold-Bug"

After Poe's popular cryptographic challenges, he wrote a treasure-hunting tale that included a gold-colored bug and cryptographic puzzles that led to a lost pirate treasure. The story, which was set in Sullivan's Island, South Carolina, had its first half published on June 21, 1843, with the complete story published a week later. It became the most successful story in Poe's lifetime, earning him a $100 prize after he submitted it to a relatively new publication in Philadelphia called the *Dollar Newspaper*. This paid for about a year of Poe's rent!

A few years after the success of "The Gold-Bug," in 1845, Poe published "The Raven." He wrote in a letter to his friend Frederick William Thomas: "'The Raven' has had a great 'run', Thomas—but I wrote it for the express purpose of running—just as I did the 'Gold-Bug', you know. The bird beat the bug, though, all hollow." Poe's bird remains unmatched, still beating his most famous tale. Nevertheless, "The Gold-Bug" was reprinted in papers throughout the country. Poe claimed that 300,000 copies of his story were circulated at the time.

The first printing of "The Gold-Bug" was accompanied with illustrations by Poe's friend, an artist named F.O.C. Darley. Darley also promised to illustrate for the magazine

Poe still hoped to launch. The popularity of "The Gold-Bug" was so significant, it was even adapted into a stage play written by Silas Steele. The play premiered at Philadelphia's American Theatre on August 8, 1843; however, it was not nearly as successful as the tale. One local newspaper published a review, stating that "Mr. Steele had a good house at his benefit on Tuesday night, and the performances were generally good. The Gold Bug, however, dragged, and was rather tedious. The frame work was well enough, but wanted filling up."

THE MORE YOU KNOW

The inventor of the popular board game Scrabble, Alfred Mosher Butts, was struck with the idea for the game while reading Poe's popular tale "The Gold-Bug." Calling his game Lexiko in 1931, he tweaked it and retitled it Criss-Cross Words. Finally, in 1948, it was redesigned and renamed Scrabble. Today, Scrabble is available in nearly thirty languages and sells roughly 1.5 million units a year.

The Prose Romances of Edgar A. Poe

After the major success of "The Gold-Bug," Poe published his second book of tales, *The Prose Romances of Edgar A. Poe*, in the hope of continuing the momentum. Advertisements for the book mentioned Poe as the author of "The Gold-Bug," *The Narrative of Arthur Gordon Pym of Nantucket*, and *Tales of the Grotesque and Arabesque*, which intended to give the book extra appeal to potential buyers. It was published in the summer of 1843 by William H. Graham, the brother of Poe's boss, George Graham of *Graham's Magazine*.

Prose romance is a type of fiction that features unbelievable or uncommon events. The two tales Poe included in this little book were "The Murders in the Rue Morgue" and "The Man That Was Used Up." While many are familiar with the former tale, the latter is lesser known. "The Man That Was Used Up" is a satirical story that follows the narrator's quest to uncover the secrets of a renowned war hero, Brevit Brigadier General John A.B.C. Smith. Upon meeting Smith, the narrator discovers that the general is a mere shell of his former self, severely injured in battle and reliant on prosthetics. This revelation serves as a critique of the glorification of war and the dehumanizing effects of technological advancements.

Poe had included "The Man That Was Used Up" in his earlier volume of works, *Tales of the Grotesque and Arabesque*, while "The Murders in the Rue Morgue" first appeared within a book: *Prose Romances*. Reviews of *Prose Romances* were quite good, but the book didn't sell well (it's not really known why). Poe was continuing on his journey to gain financial stability with his writing, and so far, publishing volumes of his own works was not proving to be the route to go. And although magazines and newspapers were the most stable outlets for his writing, they just didn't pay enough.

THE MORE YOU KNOW

Poe noted on the cover of *The Prose Romances of Edgar A. Poe* that this was "NO. 1," intending to launch a serial edition of published tales. Unfortunately, due to the unsuccessful sales of the book (which cost readers 12½ cents per copy), a second installment never came to be. It is not certain how many copies were printed initially, but fourteen exist today. It is likely that several original copies perished in a fire that occurred at the publisher's office in 1845.

The Lecture Tour

Poe gained another source of both fame and income in November 1843 when the William Wirt Institute Lectures and Debates included him in their programming. Lectures were becoming quite a popular form of performance art in the nineteenth century, especially for writers. More railroads were starting to be built in America around this time, allowing high-minded lecturers to travel to and from towns and cities, educating the population. The topic of Poe's lecture was American poetry, which audiences were eager to hear Poe speak about. Newspapers advertised the lecture calling Poe a "born poet" with a mind that was "stamped with the impress of genius." The lecture took place in the Juliana Street Church in Philadelphia, which overflowed with people. Hundreds of additional listeners who couldn't gain admission gathered outside the church.

Papers praised the lecture in the days after, and Poe realized that there was a demand for not only his poetry and prose but also now his talks. Other prominent literary figures such as Ralph Waldo Emerson and Margaret Fuller were joining the lecture circuit, so why shouldn't he? Maybe it was an inherent stage presence, passed down from his actor parents, that made Poe's lectures so enthralling, or perhaps it was his captivating genius that drew audiences.

Regardless, he commanded audiences with his melodic voice and brilliant eloquence. From 1843 until his death in 1849, Poe lectured in cities throughout the country, including Philadelphia, Boston, New York, and Richmond, as well as Lowell, Massachusetts, and Providence, Rhode Island.

While Poe used the lecture platform to promote his own works, he nodded to the works of a few other writers too. His lectures also included harsh critiques of his contemporaries—unsurprising from the Tomahawk Man himself! The lectures gave Poe a slightly steadier income and allowed him to gain subscribers to his literary magazine (an idea he was still nurturing). Poe's passion for the literary arts was evident on these tours. One reporter for the *Delaware State Journal* wrote: "The lecture was an eloquent production eloquently delivered by Edgar A. Poe, Esq. of Philadelphia and at present editorially connected with that best and most popular of our lighter monthlies—Graham's Magazine. His theme was the *'Poetry of America'*—*itself* a topic particularly appropriate to one who has himself acquitted so honorable a place among the Poets of the land, and who has proven himself to possess in no small degree the high qualifications he demands in his brethren of the inspired pen. Mr. Poe is also well known as a fearless and perhaps somewhat severe *critic* of American Poesy and has not unfrequently brought down upon himself the wrath of many of the 'genus irritable.'"

THE MORE YOU KNOW

Poe made his final public appearance for a lecture at the Exchange Hotel in Richmond, Virginia, on September 24, 1849. One audience member recalled, "There was little variation and much sadness in the intonations of his voice—yet this very sadness was so completely in harmony with his history as to excite on the part of this community a deep interest in him both as a lecturer and reader." Poe died two weeks later.

"The Balloon Hoax"

On April 13, 1844, this headline appeared in New York's *The Sun*: "ASTOUNDING INTELLIGENCE BY PRIVATE EXPRESS FROM CHARLESTON VIA NORFOLK!—THE ATLANTIC OCEAN CROSSED IN THREE DAYS!!—ARRIVAL AT SULLIVAN'S ISLAND OF A STEERING BALLOON INVENTED BY MR. MONCK MASON!!" What followed was the account of an extraordinary journey across the Atlantic Ocean by eight men in a "steering balloon," which flew from England to Charleston, South Carolina. The article was credited to an "anonymous informant."

A crowd surrounded *The Sun*'s building, waiting to get their hands on a copy of the paper. Little did they know this was just a hoax perpetrated by none other than Edgar Allan Poe. Poe and his wife, Virginia, had just made their way to New York from Philadelphia, preparing to move there permanently, with Maria Clemm joining them in the following weeks. Poe's balloon hoax served as a fitting announcement that the master of sensationalistic stories had arrived in the city. Poe's story was accompanied by an engraving of the incredible machine that completed the fictional journey. Readers marveled at this technological advancement, unlike anything that existed at the time . . . only to find out that it was fake.

Poe knew how to get his work read. He maintained the belief that to be appreciated, one needs to be read, and he knew that in order to be read, he had to create works worth reading (even if they were misleading). Poe's story was believable because of the great detail he used to describe the balloon, the technology that piloted it, and even the accounts of those who took part in the adventure. Poe combined his knowledge of science, his creativity, and his ability to write convincing fiction to hook the public.

LITERARY CONNECTIONS

It's possible that Jules Verne was inspired by "The Balloon Hoax" when he wrote his 1863 novel *Five Weeks in a Balloon*, whose plot features three men exploring Africa in a hot air balloon. Verne was open about Poe's influence on his work, especially having written a sequel to Poe's only novel. Poe's recognition as a pioneer of science fiction links back to works like "The Balloon Hoax."

Opening Lines of "The Balloon Hoax"

The great problem is at length solved. The air, as well as the earth and the ocean, has been subdued by Science, and will become a common and convenient highway for mankind. *The Atlantic has been actually crossed in a Balloon;* and this too without difficulty—without any great apparent danger—with thorough control of the machine—and in the inconceivably brief period of Seventy-five hours from shore to shore! By the energy of an agent at Charleston, S. C., we are enabled to be the first to furnish the public with a detailed account of this most extraordinary voyage, which was performed between Saturday 6th instant, at 11 A. M., and 2 P. M. on Tuesday the 9th inst.: by Sir Everard Bringhurst; Mr. Osborne, a nephew of Lord Bentinck's; Mr. Monck Mason and Mr. Robert Holland, the well-known aeronauts; Mr. Harrison Ainsworth, author of Jack Sheppard, &c.; and Mr. Henson, the projector of the late unsuccessful flying machine—with two seamen from Woolwich—in all eight persons. The particulars furnished below may be relied on as authentic and accurate in every respect, as, with slight exception, they are copied *verbatim* from the joint diaries of Mr. Monck Mason and Mr. Harrison Ainsworth, to whose politeness our agent is also indebted for much verbal information respecting the balloon itself, its construction, and other matters of interest. The only alteration in the MS. received has been made for the purpose of throwing the hurried account of our agent, Mr. Forsyth, in a connected and intelligible form.

New York

The Poe family had resided in New York briefly, from 1837 to 1838, before they settled in Philadelphia. In 1844, Poe moved his family back to New York, where they would live the rest of their lives together. Shortly after the publication of "The Balloon Hoax," the family found lodging in a two-story farmhouse owned by Patrick and Mary Brennan. The farmhouse sat on about 200 acres along the Hudson River, in a rural part of New York. It was in this farmhouse that Poe finalized his greatest poem, "The Raven," while the Brennan's young daughter, Martha, sat under Poe's desk and arranged his manuscripts as he wrote.

New York was the center of the literati (educated people interested in literature and the arts) of the nineteenth century. Poe only briefly entered the circles of these high-minded people before becoming an outcast after a scandal involving him and a few literary ladies, in addition to some letters (more on this later!). While living in New York, Poe published tales such as "The Premature Burial," "The Oblong Box," "The Purloined Letter," "Some Words with a Mummy," "The Facts in the Case of M. Valdemar," "The Cask of Amontillado," and "Hop-Frog." Besides his famous raven poem, Poe published a number of poems while living in New York, including "Eulalie," "Ulalume," "The Bells," "Eldorado," and "Annabel Lee."

Poe found more editorial work in New York while he continued to make money from his lectures and sales of his writings. Unfortunately, all this effort barely made him enough to support his mother-in-law and sick wife, who was nearing the final stages of her disease. Despite the family's struggles, Poe worked as hard as he could to keep them all afloat.

THE MORE YOU KNOW

Martha Brennan was about ten years old when the Poes moved into her home. She recalled that Mr. Poe "was the greatest of husbands and devoted to his invalid wife. Frequently when she was weaker than usual, he carried her tenderly from her room to the dinner table and satisfied her every whim." Martha described Poe as a "shy, solitary, taciturn sort of man, fond of rambling down in the woods, between the house and the river, and sitting for hours upon a certain stump on the edge of the bank of the river." While the Brennan farmhouse is no longer standing, two different plaques mark its approximate location at 255 and 215 West 84th Street, commemorating the site where Edgar Allan Poe penned his most famous poem.

Evening Mirror

After settling in New York in 1844, Poe joined the staff of the newly named *Evening Mirror* in October of that year. He hadn't worked for a newspaper since resigning from *Graham's Magazine* in 1842. His job at the *Mirror* was critic and assistant editor, which paid him a modest $15 per week. Poe was hired by Nathaniel Parker Willis, who was part owner of the *Mirror*. Willis was a poet and critic himself, as well as a travel essayist. He was the highest paid magazine writer in the country.

The *Evening Mirror* was preceded by a weekly paper, the *New-York Mirror*, in 1823, followed by the *New Mirror* in 1843. Its final incarnation was the *Evening Mirror*, a daily paper that lasted from 1844 to 1898. Poe and Willis shared an interest they both published multiple articles about in *Evening Mirror*: getting authors paid decently for their work. In one article Poe published (emphasizing how the lack of an international copyright law financially affected all writers), he wrote, "How we rob foreign authors, and how we argue in our legislative halls that it is an economical thing for us to pick the foreign pocket, are points too well understood to need discussion—but there are still found individuals who ask, innocently enough, in what manner the want of the International Law affects the pecuniary interest of the native American. The man who asks the question should first write a book or a magazine article, and then offer it to a publisher for sale."

Poe worked at the *Mirror* only for a few months before he moved on to a job with a different magazine. After leaving the *Mirror*, he would occasionally run into Willis on the streets of New York, but that was about the extent of their association. Mutual friends stated that the men despised each other, but Willis attended the funeral of Poe's wife in 1847. However they might have felt about each other, Poe gave Willis's magazine its claim to fame with the publication of one of America's greatest poems.

───────── **THE MORE YOU KNOW** ─────────

In response to an article that was circulating regarding the ill-health and poverty of Edgar Allan Poe and his wife, Virginia, Nathaniel Parker Willis responded by publishing a back-handed defense. In it, Willis suggested the idea for a "Hospital for Disabled Labourers with the Brain," using Poe as the perfect example of someone such an institution would benefit. Essentially, Willis accepted the rumors that Poe was mentally unwell but argued that he was a hardworking genius who deserved a chance. Willis also gave insight into Poe's drinking habits by stating that Poe would often show up at the *Mirror* offices acting quite drunk but not at all intoxicated. Willis observed that a single glass of wine would produce this effect on Poe. Poe didn't need to drink much to become inebriated.

"The Raven"

Before Poe left the *Evening Mirror,* he published his greatest poem, "The Raven," in the January 29, 1845 issue. While Poe only made about $9 for the poem—about $370 today—it was an instant success. Newspapers and magazines across the country republished the poem in their own periodicals. Readers everywhere quoted lines from the poem, especially those with the refrain, "Nevermore." Poe became so popular over the poem that he would be recognized on the street by children who would chase him with sticks to whack his heels. Poe ignored them before turning around and shouting "Nevermore!" as they ran away laughing.

"The Raven" explores the depths of loss, despair, and grief. When a raven interrupts the narrator's grieving over his lost love, he counts on the bird to offer some kind of hopeful message. When the raven's only reply is "Nevermore," the narrator descends into rage and madness. Scholars agree that the themes of "The Raven" reflect Poe's headspace at the time he wrote it. It is important to remember that while Poe was writing this poem, his wife was slowly dying from tuberculosis.

"The Raven" is seen as one of the prime examples of American poetry. Today, Edgar Allan Poe remains synonymous with his ebony bird.

About a year after the publication of "The Raven," Poe published "The Philosophy of Composition," which explains his theory on the writing process. In it, he said that "The Raven" was written more mechanically than creatively: "For my own part, I have neither sympathy with the repugnance alluded to, nor, at any time, the least difficulty in recalling to mind the progressive steps of any of my compositions, and, since the interest of an analysis or reconstruction, such as I have considered a desideratum, is quite independent of any real or fancied interest in the thing analysed, it will not be regarded as a breach of decorum on my part to show the modus operandi by which some one of my own works was put together. I select 'The Raven' as most generally known. It is my design to render it manifest that no one point in its composition is referable either to accident or intuition—that the work proceeded step by step, to its completion, with the precision and rigid consequence of a mathematical problem."

From "The Raven"

"Prophet!" said I, "thing of evil!—prophet still,
  if bird or devil!
By that Heaven that bends above us—by that God
  we both adore—
Tell this soul with sorrow laden if, within the
  distant Aidenn,
It shall clasp a sainted maiden whom the angels
  name Lenore—
Clasp a rare and radiant maiden whom the
  angels name Lenore."
Quoth the Raven "Nevermore."

"Be that word our sign of parting, bird or fiend!"
  I shrieked, upstarting—
"Get thee back into the tempest and the Night's
  Plutonian shore!
Leave no black plume as a token of that lie thy soul
  hath spoken!
Leave my loneliness unbroken!—quit the bust above my
  door!
Take thy beak from out my heart, and take thy
  form from off my door!"
Quoth the Raven "Nevermore."

And the Raven, never flitting, still is sitting,
  still is sitting
On the pallid bust of Pallas just above my
  chamber door;
And his eyes have all the seeming of a demon's
  that is dreaming,
And the lamp-light o'er him streaming throws his
  shadow on the floor;
And my soul from out that shadow that lies
  floating on the floor
Shall be lifted—nevermore!

Broadway Journal

The *Broadway Journal* was established in New York in 1844 by two literary men, Charles Frederick Briggs and John Bisco. The magazine was shaky from the start, and the owners fell into significant financial trouble. To save the publication, they recruited Edgar Allan Poe, hoping that his literary reputation would keep it from going completely under. Given Poe's status after the publication of "The Raven," he was able to bring much-needed attention to the *Journal*.

The *Broadway Journal* was a weekly periodical, published every Saturday. It contained about sixteen pages of literature, which included poetry, criticism, reviews, short stories, and articles. The *Broadway Journal* is where Poe published some flirty poems to another writer, Frances Osgood (more on this later!).

With Poe, Briggs, and Bisco all being part owners of the *Broadway Journal*, they struggled to keep it afloat. Briggs attempted to buy out Bisco to get more of the profit for himself but ended up leaving the magazine altogether. Now, Poe and Bisco were sole owners, and Poe decided to borrow money from a friend to buy out his partner and gain full ownership. In October 1845, Edgar Allan Poe became the sole proprietor of the *Broadway Journal*. This was the only publication that Poe had complete ownership of in his lifetime, finally fulfilling his dream of owning his own magazine. However, the magazine's financial straits proved too much, and it folded once and for all in early 1846. Poe claimed that he "never regarded it as more than a temporary adjunct to other designs."

LITERARY CONNECTIONS

One of Poe's criticisms in the *Broadway Journal* targeted the much-loved American poet Henry Wadsworth Longfellow, accusing him of plagiarism. Longfellow refused to entertain the accusations, and an anonymous critic signed "Outis" (a Classical Greek word meaning "nobody") started sending submissions to the *Journal* accusing Poe himself of being a plagiarist. Scholars believe that the anonymous "Outis" was actually Poe himself trying to keep the literary volley going in order to gain attention and readers. After all, he was famous for hoaxes!

Frances Osgood

One of Edgar Allan Poe's most intense literary flirtations involved a married woman named Frances Sargent Osgood. Frances was the wife of a portrait painter named Samuel Stillman Osgood and the mother of three children. They lived in New York, but Samuel often traveled for work, leaving Frances and their daughters at home. Frances Osgood was a poet of some renown, as well as an essayist and a children's author. Her work caught Poe's attention, and he praised it in his published reviews and his lectures. They met shortly after the publication of Poe's "The Raven" in March 1845 when Frances sought the introduction after reading Poe's flattering comments about her work.

Poe and Osgood met at the Astor House, which was a luxury hotel in New York. (The building was located in what is known today as Lower Manhattan; the hotel no longer exists, having been demolished in the early twentieth century). Osgood recalled her first impression of Poe, "With his proud and beautiful head erect, his dark eyes flashing with the elective light of feeling and of thought, a peculiar, and inimitable blending of sweetness and hauteur in his expression and manner, he greeted me, calmly, gravely, almost coldly; yet with so marked an earnestness that I could not help being deeply impressed by it. From that moment until his death we were friends; although we met only during the first year of our acquaintance." While Osgood claimed they were friends until his death in 1849, this wasn't exactly true.

The nature of their relationship is up for much debate. The two publicly exchanged flirtatious poetry in the *Broadway Journal*—despite the fact they were both married to other people. Osgood was even a frequent visitor to Poe's house, where she befriended his wife, Virginia, and Poe sat for her husband, Samuel, to have his portrait painted. So, the relationship wasn't a secret to anyone, but a scandal involving some private letters would not only end their friendship and rumored affair the following year (at least from Poe's perspective) but also completely tarnish Poe's reputation among the literati.

LITERARY CONNECTIONS

Poe published a valentine to Frances Osgood in the *Evening Mirror* in February 1846 under the title "To Her Whose Name Is Written Below." Frances Sargent Osgood's full name was hidden in the poem (her middle name was spelled incorrectly). You can find it by taking the first letter of the first line, the second letter of the second line, the third letter of the third line, etc. There is a question of whether this poem, subsequently titled "A Valentine," was *actually* written by Poe or if it was written by his wife, Virginia (more on this later).

"A Valentine" ("To Her Whose Name Is Written Below")

For her these lines are penned, whose luminous eyes,
   Bright and expressive as the stars of Leda,
Shall find her own sweet name that, nestling, lies
   Upon this page, enwrapped from every reader.
Search narrowly these words, which hold a treasure
   Divine—a talisman—an amulet
That must be worn *at heart*. Search well the measure—
   The words—the letters themselves. Do not forget
The smallest point, or you may lose your labor.
   And yet there is in this no Gordian knot,
Which one might not undo without a sabre.
   If one could merely comprehend the plot
Upon the open page, on which are peering
   Such sweet eyes now, there lies, I say perdu,
A musical name, oft uttered in the hearing
   Of poets, by poets—for the name is a poet's, too,
In common sequence set, the letters lying,
   Compose a sound delighting all to hear.
Ah, this you'd have no trouble in descrying,
   Were you not something, of a dunce, my dear:
   And now I leave these riddles to their seer.

Tales & The Raven and Other Poems

In 1845, Edgar Allan Poe had both an edition of prose and a volume of poetry published in New York by the publisher Wiley & Putnam. The book of prose, simply titled *Tales*, was published in the summer of that year and included a selection of short stories chosen by a man named Evert Augustus Duyckinck, a prominent figure in literature at the time. He was responsible for editing Wiley & Putnam's Library of American Books series, which led to his connection with Poe. A critical success, *Tales* included "The Gold-Bug," "The Black Cat," "The Fall of the House of Usher," and Poe's three Dupin tales. This was technically Poe's fourth book of prose.

The book of poetry (his fourth) was published on November 19, 1845, and titled *The Raven and Other Poems*. Poe made sure this new edition of poetry featured his celebrated literary achievement "The Raven." He dedicated the volume to Elizabeth Barrett Browning, an English poet who was popular in the United States. Poe had given Browning's *A Drama of Exile: And Other Poems* a favorable review in the *Broadway Journal* and was a fan of her work.

About 1,500 copies of each book were issued, and they sold quite well. Some of the poems included in *The Raven* and *Other Poems* were "Lenore," "Israfel," "Dream-Land," "The City in the Sea," "The Conqueror Worm," and of course, "The Raven." The following year, *Tales* and *The Raven and Other Poems* were bound together in hardcovers and sold as a double volume for $1 each. Today, these first editions are very rare and sell for thousands of dollars.

LITERARY CONNECTIONS

One of the poems included in Elizabeth Barrett Browning's *A Drama of Exile: And Other Poems* (published in 1844) was "Lady Geraldine's Courtship." Edgar Allan Poe heavily borrowed from Browning's poem in his own writing, particularly the meter and rhyme scheme for "The Raven." This is chiefly the reason why he dedicated *The Raven and Other Poems* to her, as an acknowledgment of her crucial inspiration for his most successful poem.

From "The City in the Sea"

LO! Death has reared himself a throne
In a strange city lying alone
Far down within the dim West,
Where the good and the bad and the worst and the best
Have gone to their eternal rest.
There shrines and palaces and towers
(Time-eaten towers that tremble not!)
Resemble nothing that is ours.
Around, by lifting winds forgot,
Resignedly beneath the sky
The melancholy waters lie.

(. . .)

But lo, a stir is in the air!
The wave—there is a movement there!
As if the towers had thrust aside,
In slightly sinking, the dull tide—
As if their tops had feebly given
A void within the filmy Heaven.
The waves have now a redder glow—
The hours are breathing faint and low—
And when, amid no earthly moans,
Down, down that town shall settle hence.
Hell, rising from a thousand thrones,
Shall do it reverence.

The Letters Scandal

Perhaps the most scandalous moment of Edgar Allan Poe's life was an exchange of letters that happened in early 1846. The instigator was a woman named Elizabeth Ellet, a writer and poet among the literary circles in New York at the time. Poe had given her work decent reviews, but she craved more than just his praises. Ellet was friends with Frances Osgood, and both women were competing for Poe's romantic affection and attention. There is no question that Poe and Osgood exchanged some rather intimate letters, but when Ellet sent Poe a love letter of her own, things got out of control.

One day while Ellet was visiting Poe and his wife, Virginia, at their home in New York, Ellet caught a glimpse of an "indiscreet" letter from Osgood to Poe, lying on his desk. On another visit to Poe's house, Ellet discovered Osgood and Virginia laughing at one of her love letters to Poe, which infuriated her. She snatched the letter from their hands and stormed out of the house. For whatever reason, she later convinced Osgood to request the return of all her letters to Poe after telling her that she saw the contents of one of them on a previous visit. Some believe Osgood was worried that the situation was going to escalate between her, Poe, and now Ellet, who were all married. So, Osgood had her friends Anne Lynch and Margaret Fuller go to Poe's house and demand her letters back.

When Poe learned that Ellet was the cause of this disturbance at his front door, he told the women that Ellet should be more concerned with her own letters to him, insinuating that hers were no less inappropriate than Osgood's. The women left with Osgood's letters, and Poe decided to collect all of Ellet's letters in a bundle and drop them off at her door.

THE MORE YOU KNOW

The ordeal got weirder. Because Poe insinuated to Ann Lynch and Margaret Fuller that Elizabeth Ellet's letters were compromising, Ellet sent her brother, William Lummis, to call on Poe at his house and demand his sister's letters back. But because Poe had already dropped them off at her house (apparently, she didn't see them before sending her brother to confront him), he couldn't hand them over. Poe turned to his acquaintance, Thomas Dunn English, for help, asking to borrow a pistol from him for self-defense. English refused, accusing him of making it all up. This angered Poe so much that he then got into a fistfight with English. Another friend broke up the fight, and tensions defused over the next few weeks.

"Ever with Thee"

With Virginia's health failing so fast, Edgar Allan Poe likely knew that February 14, 1846, would be the last Valentine's Day he would spend with his wife. And it was. Virginia's only authenticated piece of writing is an acrostic poem she wrote as a valentine to Poe, which bears Edgar Allan Poe's name along the left margin:

```
Ever with thee I wish to roam—
Dearest my life is thine.
Give me a cottage for my home
And a rich old cypress vine,
Removed from the world with its sin and care
And the tattling of many tongues.
Love alone shall guide us when we are there—
Love shall heal my weakened lungs;
And oh, the tranquil hours we'll spend,
Never wishing that others may see!
Perfect ease we'll enjoy, without thinking to lend
Ourselves to the world and its glee—
Ever peaceful and blissful we'll be.
```

In this poem, Virginia expressed what Poe's love truly meant to her and the gratitude she felt for her husband despite the poverty they endured for most of their marriage. She emphasized her lack of need for wealth or society but rather her need for peace and seclusion with her husband.

Together, their love provided them with all the riches they could ever ask for.

The "tattling of many tongues" most likely refers to the letters scandal with Ellet and Osgood. On her deathbed, Virginia claimed that Ellet had been her murderer because of the unnecessary anguish Ellet caused her and her husband. She died less than a year after writing the poem.

────────── LITERARY CONNECTIONS ──────────

What's peculiar about Virginia Poe's Valentine's Day poem to her husband is that the handwriting in the original manuscript is nearly an exact match to the handwriting in the original manuscript of the Valentine's Day poem written to Frances Osgood (explored previously in this book). The poem that Poe's wife wrote for him was written at the same time as the poem to Osgood, and they are even written on similar floral paper. The language in the Osgood poem is unlike anything Poe was writing at the time. If the Osgood poem was actually written by Virginia, this could be the reason why Osgood is called a "dunce" in one of the last lines, given the controversy brewing around the time the poem was written.

─────────────── ──○── ───────────────

"Give Me a Cottage"

To escape the literati and their scandals, Poe moved his family in 1846 out of the chaotic city and into a small Dutch farm cottage on Kingsbridge Road in Fordham (now the Bronx), honoring his wife's request to "Give [her] a cottage for [her] home." At the time, the area surrounding the cottage was all countryside. It sat on top of a large hill surrounded by farmland, fruit trees, and gardens, which were all that could be seen for miles. Poe also moved his family there to help treat his wife's consumption: Fresh air was recommended by physicians to help cure the disease.

The cottage was owned by a man named John Valentine, who rented it out to Poe for $100 a year. Valentine also owned some of the surrounding farmland. Poe received many important friends and colleagues at the cottage, who all commented that it was such a small, impoverished dwelling, yet so cozy and homey. Maria Clemm kept it very neat, and although the family had very little furniture or possessions, it was decorated quite tastefully.

Edgar Allan Poe had some of his happiest moments in Fordham. But it was also in this cottage that the Poe family found their final home together. Virginia would die less than a year after moving in, and Poe would follow her to the grave only two short years later.

Edgar Allan Poe befriended some of the Jesuit priests at St. John's College near his Fordham cottage. Poe commented that they "were highly cultivated gentlemen and scholars" who "smoked, drank, and played cards like gentlemen, and never said a word about religion." Poe even sponsored the baptism of a baby born to a local family, who named the boy after Poe. Instead of "Edgar Allan," Poe suggested "Edgar Albert," since he detested his namesake (his foster father) and said that the name Allan had brought him nothing but bad luck. And so, Edgar Allan Poe sponsored the baptism of Edgar Albert at the parish of St. John's College.

Libel

The secluded cottage out in Fordham couldn't entirely shelter Edgar Allan Poe from the problems that persisted from the letters debacle. Poe's reputation had been completely tarnished, since Osgood and Ellet threw all the blame on him to make themselves appear the victims. In reality, they were the ones sending Poe the unsolicited love letters. Regardless, the gossip didn't help Poe's case when Thomas Dunn English, the man Poe had a fistfight with after the letters scandal escalated, published scathing articles about him in the *Evening Mirror*. The magazine was under the editorship of a man named Hiram Fuller at this time.

For his part, in his Literati of New York City lecture series, Poe had called English an uneducated hack of a writer. In English's subsequent article, which in an introduction he noted was severe, he called Poe an immoral drunkard who went out of his way to do immoral things, and a poor, sad imbecile. He also said Poe was a "quack in literature." Additionally, English wrote that Poe tricked him into loaning him money and that Poe had once been charged with forgery. Apparently, these were the false charges that sent Poe over the edge.

Poe replied with legal action aimed more at Fuller for publishing such slanders than at English for writing them.

Poe hired New York lawyer Enoch L. Fancher to take his case. Together, they went after the *Mirror* for the comments about Poe committing forgery and taking money under false pretenses. Poe won the suit, which awarded him $225.

─────────── **LITERARY CONNECTIONS** ───────────

Almost immediately after his libel case was settled, Poe published one of his most well-known short stories, "The Cask of Amontillado," in November 1846. The story is one of Poe's prime examples of a revenge tale, and many scholars believe it was written in the context of Poe's relationship with Thomas Dunn English. It is also one of Poe's only tales where the narrator gets away with his crime. Three years prior, English's pro-temperance novel *The Doom of the Drinker* had been published in serialized form. The novel features a character named Walter Woolfe, a superior writer who falls victim to the treacheries of alcohol, which comes to define his life. English intended this character to be a caricature of Edgar Allan Poe.

From "The Cask of Amontillado"

The thousand injuries of Fortunato I had borne as I best could, but when he ventured upon insult I vowed revenge. You, who so well know the nature of my soul, will not suppose, however, that I gave utterance to a threat. *At length* I would be avenged; this was a point definitively settled—but the very definitiveness with which it was resolved precluded the idea of risk. I must not only punish but punish with impunity. A wrong is unredressed when retribution overtakes its redresser. It is equally unredressed when the avenger fails to make himself felt as such to him who has done the wrong.

Poe's Private Life

Despite the grim portrayal of Edgar Allan Poe that English was circulating in the *Evening Mirror*, Poe sought a life of peace and happiness that reflected quite the opposite. While he may have been harsh or difficult to work with professionally, in his personal life his behavior was described as quite ordinary and affectionate. He relished every moment he could with his sick wife and continued to master his craft and write prolifically.

Beyond his writing, Poe cherished life's simple pleasures. He would often play the flute, accompanying Virginia as she sang or played the piano or harp. Together, they spent hours in the garden, where Poe would climb the cherry trees and toss fruit down to his wife, who caught it in her apron. Maria Clemm would then bake pies with the fruit. One day, the couple engaged in a game of leapfrog, during which Poe split his pants. Virginia burst into laughter, and they then shared a hearty chuckle over the incident. Poe enjoyed long, solitary walks in the woods, and he found quite a bit of joy and peace in his life despite the many trials that burdened him.

Poe also enjoyed simple hobbies. He would make traps to catch wild birds, admiring them in their cages before releasing them back into the wild. His passion for nature extended to gardening, and friends often praised the rare, vibrant dahlias he cultivated in the garden outside his cottage. The image of Poe hunched over his desk with a raven perched on his shoulder as lightning flashes through the window may be popular today, but it is a mere caricature. In reality, Poe lived a quiet domestic life with his wife and mother-in-law and their pet cat, Catterina.

THE MORE YOU KNOW

Many of the recollections of Edgar Allan Poe's home life come from the friends who were frequent visitors. They cared deeply for Poe and his family and even helped them through their darkest times, donating food and provisions to keep them alive and comfortable.

Catterina

One of Poe's lesser-known but equally important muses was his beloved cat, Catterina, a female tortoiseshell that joined the family at some point when they were living in Philadelphia. She could have been a stray kitten they took in, or perhaps she was a gift from a friend. Either way, she was a cherished member of the family. After Poe and Virginia moved to New York from Philadelphia and before Poe could afford to move Maria Clemm and Catterina in with them, he wrote to Maria, "You can't imagine how much we both do miss you. Sissy [Virginia] had a hearty cry last night, because you and Catterina weren't here....Give our best love to Catterina."

Because of his short story "The Black Cat," some might think Poe had an aversion to felines. But he had deep affection for his own pet cat. Catterina would perch on Poe's shoulder as he wrote, and he'd give her a scratch under the chin between dips of his pen in the inkwell. He would also get up at all hours of the night to let her in and out of the house. And when Poe was away from home, Catterina refused to eat.

Catterina also had an important role, which she dutifully fulfilled and for which she is most known. As Virginia was in the final stages of her illness, Poe was unemployed and very poor. Before friends stepped in to help the family, Virginia kept warm with nothing but Poe's old military frock coat and Catterina, who would curl up on Virginia's chest and help keep her warm. After Edgar Allan Poe's mysterious death in 1849, Maria Clemm and Catterina were the only surviving members of the family. However, just days after Poe died, Maria found Catterina deceased from an unknown cause. The Poe family had the treasured cat for around thirteen years before she passed away.

LITERARY CONNECTIONS

Edgar Allan Poe's story "The Black Cat" was partly responsible for bringing him posthumous acclaim in France. The French poet Charles Baudelaire had read a translation of the story by Isabelle Meunier, published in *La Démocratie pacifique* on January 27, 1847. Baudelaire read it and immediately became a fan of Poe's works. He memorized the entire story and could recite it for his friends. Baudelaire was later responsible for translating Poe's works into French, bringing him a large audience abroad.

"Deep in Earth"

The day before Virginia's death, Poe wrote to their friend and nurse, Marie Louise Shew: "My poor Virginia still lives, although failing fast and now suffering much pain." Mary Starr, Poe's former Baltimore love who Virginia used to deliver his love letters to, visited the cottage on the eve of Virginia's death. Mary sat on one side of a big armchair where Virginia was placed while Poe sat on the other side. Virginia put Mary's hand in Poe's and asked her to be a friend to him, stating that "he always loved you."

It was a bitterly cold Saturday on January 30, 1847, when Virginia Eliza Clemm Poe took her final breath at twenty-four years old. She was surrounded by her loving husband, her mother, and likely her nurse, Marie Louise Shew, who immediately came to their aid after receiving Poe's letter. A postmortem watercolor portrait was painted of Virginia by an unknown artist. It is the only authenticated image of Virginia that exists. Along with the financial assistance of Mary Starr, Shew used her own money to purchase Virginia's coffin and burial clothes, as well as Poe's mourning clothes.

The wake and funeral took place at the small cottage in Fordham three days after Virginia's death. In attendance were some of Poe's closest literary friends and even some of the neighbors. Virginia was interred in the family vault of their landlord, John Valentine. Days after Virginia was laid to rest, Poe wrote a couplet on the back of a manuscript copy of his poem "Eulalie" (a poem that celebrates a joyous marriage). The couplet has quite the opposite tone to "Eulalie": "Deep in earth my love is lying/And I must weep alone." According to those around him, Poe was absolutely shattered, and he never quite recovered after Virginia died. He turned his attention and affection to Shew, who was now attending to his own medical needs.

THE MORE YOU KNOW

Neighbors of the cottage in Fordham recalled seeing Edgar Allan Poe at all hours of the day and night weeping at his wife's grave. He kept it supplied with fresh flowers. While herself dealing with the death of her daughter, Maria Clemm soon became concerned for the health of her son-in-law.

The Beloved Physician

Marie Louise Shew was a medically trained nurse who was summoned to the Poe family's cottage in the winter of 1846 after a mutual friend told her of the deplorable conditions they were living in. Shew, along with some other friends of the Poe family, was able to secure Virginia proper bedding and warm clothing. She was a savior to the Poe family, and Poe became quite infatuated with her.

Shew tried to dampen the fervor of Poe's feelings, as her love life was complicated enough! Separated from her husband, Shew was still living with him while entangled in an affair with a clergyman named Roland Houghton. She eventually became pregnant (presumably with Houghton's child), divorced her husband, and married Houghton. However, despite not returning Poe's feelings, she supported his family devotedly and shifted her professional attention to him when he became sick frequently after his wife's death, up until his own death two years later.

Although Shew was a savior to the Poe family, she actually lived a rather dark and sinister life in the decades following her association with them. In 1876, she was nearly prosecuted for the murder of her son's mistress, Mary Stanley. Having been Stanley's medical attendant during the birth of Stanley's child, Shew failed to call a doctor until it was obviously too late. Stanley died shortly after giving birth, and Shew arranged an immediate burial without a death certificate. The jury at the inquest ruled in her favor, however, and Shew escaped any charges. She died on September 3, 1877, less than a year after the inquest took place.

LITERARY CONNECTIONS

Around April 1847, Poe composed a very personal poem for Marie Louise Shew titled "The Beloved Physician" and was offered $20 for its publication. Shew paid him $25 to *prevent* its publication, claiming that "every body would know who it was addressed to and it was so very personal and complimentary I dreaded the ordeal." This was one of two poems of Poe's that he dedicated to his beloved nurse. The poem was never published; all that remains are fragments written on a manuscript owned by Shew.

"The Beloved Physician" (Existing Fragments)

The pulse beats ten and intermits;
God nerve the soul that ne'er forgets
In calm or storm, by night or day,
Its steady toil, its loyalty.

The pulse beats ten and intermits;
God shield the soul that ne'er forgets.

The pulse beats ten and intermits;
God guide the soul that ne'er forgets.

So tired, so weary,
The soft head bows, the sweet eyes close,
The faithful heart yields to repose.

"I Became Insane, with Long Intervals of Horrible Sanity"

One of Edgar Allan Poe's most celebrated quotes is often taken out of context. The quote, "I became insane, with long intervals of horrible sanity," reflects the general myth that Poe was a madman like the characters in his stories. However, this line comes from a letter written to one of Poe's friends about the tragic illness and death of his young wife, Virginia. The friend, George Washington Eveleth, was a fan who lived in Maine. He started a correspondence with the author in 1845 that lasted until Poe's death in 1849.

In the letter, Poe writes: "Six years ago, a wife, whom I loved as no man ever loved before, ruptured a blood-vessel in singing. Her life was despaired of. I took leave of her forever & underwent all the agonies of her death. She recovered partially and I again hoped. At the end of a year the vessel broke again—I went through precisely the same scene. Again in about a year afterward. Then again—again—again & even once again at varying intervals. Each time I felt all the agonies of her death—and at each accession of the disorder I loved her more dearly & clung to her life with more desperate pertinacity. But I am constitutionally sensitive—nervous in a very unusual degree. I became insane, with long intervals of horrible sanity."

In the full context of the quote, the long illness that slowly took the life of his wife was the reason that Poe was emotionally and mentally unwell. He had to watch helplessly as the woman he loved was being taken away from him by a disease that had no known cure. Out of context, most readers think that with this quote, Poe was literally describing himself as insane.

LITERARY CONNECTIONS

Virginia Poe's battle with consumption (tuberculosis), where she recovered and relapsed constantly, is thought to explain the recurring theme of female resurrection in Edgar Allan Poe's work. A prime example can be found in his short story, "Ligeia," where the narrator's beloved wife, Ligeia, dies. He marries a second wife, Lady Rowena, and she too dies. The narrator sits with the corpse of Lady Rowena only to see her slowly come back to life, transformed into Ligeia.

Lesions on the Brain

The only professional insight that can be gained into Edgar Allan Poe's physical health in the final two years of his life comes from his nurse, Marie Louise Shew. Shew was acquainted with many doctors who she had examine Poe during this time to give their diagnoses of whatever was ailing him. In March 1847, Shew took Poe to Dr. Valentine Mott of the New York University School of Medicine after she came to the conclusion that he had lesions on one side of his brain. She also claimed that he had an irregular pulse, which beat only ten times before it suspended, starting up again intermittently. There's no record that Mott had a different opinion of what was ailing Poe.

Shew's diagnoses came after she witnessed Poe's inability to have stimulants like alcohol without "producing insanity." She also claimed that she had to be cautious administering him medicine, which would also aggravate his system. In May 1848, another doctor, named John W. Francis, examined Poe at Shew's home, and he diagnosed Poe as having heart disease. Poe later claimed that his "nervous disorder" deceived the physician and that he didn't actually have heart disease. Shew believed that Poe's ailments were brought on by the extreme suffering of "mind and body" that he endured for most of his life.

Given the medical resources of the time, some think these diagnoses were plausible: They were made by professionals with the knowledge and technology available to them in the mid-nineteenth century. Their diagnoses could serve as clues to help connect some of the dots in Edgar Allan Poe's mysterious death, which would occur within just a couple of years.

THE MORE YOU KNOW

When Poe was exhumed from his grave twenty-six years after his death, his coffin collapsed and his full skeleton was visible to the gravediggers. One of the workers noticed some kind of mass rolling around inside the skull. Newspapers reported the incident, claiming that the brain of the genius poet remained in his skull, though shriveled, decades after his death. Modern science says that organs don't last nearly that long after death. However, a brain tumor might have calcified, causing the clump the gravedigger noticed. This anecdote could corroborate Shew's diagnosis of lesions on Poe's brain. Unfortunately, the testimonies regarding Poe's exhumation are subject to fabrication. The truth may never be known for sure!

"The Bells"

Marie Louise Shew not only inspired poetry by Edgar Allan Poe but also helped him write it. One of Poe's most famous poems, "The Bells," was coauthored by Shew. It happened one evening when Poe visited Shew at her house in Greenwich Village, New York. She recalled, "He came in and said, 'Marie Louise, I have to write a poem. I have no feeling, no sentiment, no inspiration—' I answered we will have supper and I will help you. So after tea had been served in a conservatory with the windows open, near a church—I playfully said, here is paper. A Bell (very jolly and sharp) rang at the corner of the street. He said 'I so dislike the noise of bells tonight. I cannot write. I have no subject. I am exhausted.' So I took his pen and wrote 'The Bells. By E. A. Poe' and I mimicked his style, and wrote the Bells, the little silver Bells and he finished each line."

When the poem was completed, Poe drafted the final copy and wrote the heading "By Mrs. M.L. Shew," since he had credited her with composing much of the contents. "The Bells" is considered Poe's finest example of onomatopoeia. As the poem is recited, the repetition and rhythm of the word "bells" nearly creates the sound of actual bells. This poem was a hit when Poe recited it at lectures in 1848 and 1849. As the bells ring through every stage of life, from childhood to death, Poe claims that death is inevitable no matter what stage of life you are in.

Poe submitted the poem to *Sartain's Union Magazine*, which was co-owned by his friend John Sartain. However, Poe kept withdrawing the submission to edit the poem and add more stanzas. Finally, when Poe was satisfied with it, Sartain paid him $15 for the manuscript. Unfortunately, Poe never saw the poem in print. It was published when the iron bells tolled after his death the following year, in the November 1849 issue of the magazine.

LITERARY CONNECTIONS

By the time Edgar Allan Poe and Marie Louise Shew wrote "The Bells" together, Shew was slowly withdrawing from Poe's life. This was in part due to a major work that Poe had been preparing to publish around this time, which Shew is believed to have read or at least heard about from Poe. The work, *Eureka: A Prose Poem*, was Poe's approach to the theory of the nature and origin of the universe, which contradicted Shew's devout Christianity. It's thought that this conflict, along with Poe's infatuation with her, pushed Shew away.

Eureka: A Prose Poem

Published in the summer of 1848, Poe's essay on cosmology was taken very seriously (by him, at least). In fact, up until his death, Poe considered it his greatest work!

The essay explores the mysteries of the universe from someone with very little scientific background. However, Poe's theories (at least some of them) were not too far off from what modern science has been able to confirm. For example, in the essay, Poe theorizes that the universe is expanding from a central point. This expansion was proven by astronomer Edwin Hubble in 1929. But because *Eureka* contradicted the theology popular at the time, its reception was mixed. Some people thought it was genius, while many others thought Poe was a lunatic.

Eureka was the final straw that broke the friendship of Poe and his nurse, Marie Louise Shew. Shew was a God-fearing, spiritual person, and she attempted to salvage Poe's faith in God during their friendship. But with *Eureka* contradicting the Christian faith, her close spiritual friends persuaded her that a relationship with Poe was just too damaging to her spiritual health. In the early summer of 1848, Shew wrote to Poe cutting all ties with him. He replied: "Can it be true Louise that you have the idea fixed in your mind to desert your unhappy and unfortunate friend and patient." *Eureka* was the last book that Edgar Allan Poe ever published. He thought it would be the book that everyone remembered him by, but readers today can hardly get through it without scratching their heads.

THE MORE YOU KNOW

Despite the ideas that Poe presented in *Eureka*, his personal religious views are up for debate. For a brief time, Poe was going to church with Marie Louise Shew, learning all the hymns and singing them quite beautifully. In his letter appealing to her to change her mind about breaking off their friendship, he claims that she had in fact restored his faith in God. In the final year of his life, Poe closed his letters to his mother-in-law, "God bless you," and he carried a Bible that she gave him, where he marked his favorite verses in pencil. Like many facets of Poe's life, it may never be known exactly where he stood on spiritual or religious matters. His love of hoaxes, satire, controversy, and sensationalism often concealed his true beliefs.

The Stylus

Although Edgar Allan Poe was going through physical and emotional torments during the last few years of his life, he still pursued his dream to establish his own literary magazine. Poe had changed the name of his prospective periodical, formerly titled *Penn Magazine*, to *The Stylus*. By the end of 1848, Poe had recovered sufficiently from the loss of his wife to direct his efforts to the magazine. While his wife was gone, he still had himself and his aunt Maria Clemm to support.

Poe wrote to his late foster mother's cousin Edward Valentine (who was quite wealthy), appealing for financial aid. In the letter, Poe wrote, "After a long and bitter struggle with illness, poverty, and the thousand evils which attend them, I find myself at length in a position to establish myself permanently, and to triumph over all difficulties, if I could but obtain, from some friend, a very little pecuniary aid." Poe continued, "I venture to throw myself upon your generosity and ask you to lend me $200. With this sum I should be able to take the first steps in an enterprise where there can be no doubt of my success, and which, if successful, would, in one or two years, ensure me fortune and very great influence. I refer to the establishment of a Magazine, for which I have already a good list of subscribers, and of which I send you a Prospectus."

Valentine never lent Poe the money, which might have been for the best in his case, since he wouldn't have seen a return; Poe was dead less than a year after writing to him. Scholars and fans alike raise the question of why Poe couldn't achieve his dream. As Poe claimed in his letter, a string of bad luck seems to have struck every time he came close to his goal. Illness, financial trouble, and the slow, agonizing death of his wife impeded every opportunity that came his way. But he remained hopeful.

THE MORE YOU KNOW

Poe's vision for *The Stylus* was totally unique for the time. He wanted the magazine to include nothing but literature, art, and drama. He planned to omit anything related to fashion, politics, or news and to focus primarily on what was most important to him. His magazine (had it ever came to be) would have been unlike anything available to readers at the time.

Lowell

Not only did Edgar Allan Poe get back to his long-anticipated magazine venture, but he also re-entered the lecture circuit. In the summer of 1848, his lecture "The Poets and Poetry of America" brought him to Lowell, Massachusetts. Newspapers the day following the lecture reported that Poe had been "deservedly listened to with much attention." Lowell became quite a significant place for Poe, primarily due to one of the city's occupants, who Poe held close to his heart: Nancy "Annie" Richmond. But the person initially responsible for connecting Poe to Lowell was a woman named Jane Locke, a minor author and poet of the time.

Locke had apparently been an admirer of Poe's for some time, assisting him financially during his wife's illness. She also wrote a few poems in tribute to Poe. Despite this, Poe's interest homed in on Annie Richmond, who, along with Locke, attended the lecture that Poe gave in their city. Afterward, he was invited to visit Annie's home, where he became acquainted with her family. Because of the relationship Poe developed with Annie, he even considered moving to Lowell with his mother-in-law to be closer to her. (It should be noted that both Jane Locke and Annie Richmond were married women, completely unavailable to Poe.)

Poe's attention to Annie angered Locke so much (apparently, she wanted her celebrity friend all to herself) that she began circulating vicious rumors about him. Poe just couldn't escape the gossipy circles of his time, which stained his reputation both during and after his life!

Poe visited Lowell at least three times in the last two years of his life. His last visit was in the late spring of 1849, when two daguerreotypes were taken of him at the same sitting, producing two slightly different pictures. Exactly which studio and photographer took the photos are unknown, but they captured a very sickly looking Poe, who would pass away just months later.

THE MORE YOU KNOW

Westford, Massachusetts (a town just 10 miles from Lowell), has not one but *two* public monuments to Edgar Allan Poe. One is a stone marker off Graniteville Road in Westford outside the farm that belonged to Nancy "Annie" Richmond's parents. The marker simply states that Poe had been in the town. A multipart monument in front of the Parish Center for the Arts titled *Waiting for Poe* was unveiled on October 29, 2023. The monument features a stone bench you can sit on next to a bronze walking stick and top hat representing those Poe would have owned. Also in bronze, a few feet away from the bench, a pensive-looking raven perches on a book.

Annie

Nancy "Annie" Richmond was a twenty-eight-year-old married woman with a young daughter when Poe entered her life. Her husband, Charles Richmond, was a wealthy paper manufacturer in Lowell. When Poe met Nancy, he became immediately enamored with her, coining her nickname, Annie, by which he addressed her during their friendship. Poe's letters to his beloved Annie became incredibly intense in only a brief period of time. He addressed her as his "*pure* beautiful angel—*wife* of my soul—to be mine hereafter & *forever in the Heavens*" within months of knowing her.

It seemed that Charles Richmond supported their friendship, either ignoring Poe's very deep sentiments and love letters to his wife or not taking them seriously. Poe also referred to Annie in these letters as "sister," which blurred the lines of romantic and familial love. Poe used the same ambiguous wording with his cousin, Virginia, before marrying her. In Annie's case, some think this could have been a way for Poe to defend himself if ever confronted about his intentions. But it's not really known what Poe's intentions toward Annie were. Others believe that in her case (as well as in Poe's other romances), he chased the unattainable, which kept his love at a safe distance.

For her part, Annie encouraged his engagement to another woman, who lived in Providence, Rhode Island. But eventually, gossip among the Lockes and Annie's family pushed Poe out of Lowell and away from his beloved Annie. Despite the gossip, she eventually took his mother-in-law, Maria Clemm, into her home and supported her for some time after Poe died.

LITERARY CONNECTIONS

After the death of her husband in 1873, Nancy Richmond legally changed her first name to Annie, the nickname Poe had given her. It was also the name he immortalized in his poem "For Annie," which he sent to her in March 1849. According to relatives, Annie's daughter, Caroline, thought her mother's commemoration of Poe's love was disrespectful to her late father.

From "For Annie"

She tenderly kissed me,
She fondly caressed,
And then I fell gently
To sleep on her breast—
Deeply to sleep
From the heaven of her breast.

When the light was extinguished,
She covered me warm,
And she prayed to the angels
To keep me from harm—
To the queen of the angels
To shield me from harm.

And I lie so composedly,
Now, in my bed,
(Knowing her love)
That you fancy me dead—
And I rest so contentedly,
Now in my bed,
(With her love at my breast)
That you fancy me dead—
That you shudder to look at me,
Thinking me dead:—

But my heart it is brighter
Than all of the many
Stars in the sky,
For it sparkles with Annie—
It glows with the light
Of the love of my Annie—
With the thought of the light
Of the eyes of my Annie.

Providence

Like Lowell, Massachusetts, Providence, Rhode Island, is a city with lesser-known ties to Edgar Allan Poe. Another similarity is the main reason for Poe's extended time there: a woman. Poe's first visit to Providence was in July 1845, just a few months after his fame soared with the publication of "The Raven." He was invited by Frances Osgood, who was staying in Providence at the time.

It was during this visit that Poe became aware of the notable poet Sarah Helen Whitman, a friend of Osgood's who lived in the city. One night, Osgood took a walk with Poe past Whitman's home. According to Poe, later that night he walked the same route alone, and this time he spotted Whitman outside. It was near midnight on that humid summer night, and the moon was nearly full. Whitman was out in the moonlight tending her rosebushes, clad all in white. She had no idea that Poe even saw her that night! Three years later, in September 1848, they began a passionate romance that lasted until December of the same year.

During those months in Providence, Poe sat for his most infamous photograph, taken under horrible circumstances (the "Ultima Thule" daguerreotype). Days later, the only known daguerreotype that Poe himself commissioned was taken (the "Whitman" daguerreotype). It was the likeness he thought represented him best. He also lectured at Howard's Hall (a popular venue downtown) before a crowd of nearly 2,000 people. Additionally, Poe and Whitman spent time at the Providence Athenaeum and Swan Point Cemetery, hiding away from Whitman's friends and family, who disapproved of her relationship with him. They became engaged briefly, but the engagement was called off, primarily due to Poe's drinking. Poe left Providence and was dead less than a year later.

LITERARY CONNECTIONS

Providence, Rhode Island, inspired one poem by Poe during his first visit in 1845 when he saw Sarah Helen Whitman illuminated by moonlight in her rose garden. The poem originally had no title, but it has come to be known as his second "To Helen." The first, mentioned previously in this book, was written for Jane Stanard ("Helen, thy beauty is to me"), and the two often get confused. Poe claimed that his poem to Whitman was inspired by a vision he had after seeing her in her rose garden.

From "To Helen" (1848)

I saw thee once—once only—years ago:
I must not say how many—but not many.
It was a July midnight; and from out
A full-orbed moon, that, like thine own soul, soaring,
Sought a precipitate pathway up through heaven,
There fell a silvery-silken veil of light,
With quietude, and sultriness, and slumber,
Upon the upturn'd faces of a thousand
Roses that grew in an enchanted garden,
Where no wind dared to stir, unless on tiptoe—
Fell on the upturn'd faces of these roses
That gave out, in return for the love-light,
Their odorous souls in an ecstatic death—
Fell on the upturn'd faces of these roses
That smiled and died in this parterre, enchanted
By thee, and by the poetry of thy presence.

Sarah Helen Whitman

I t's argued that one of the most intense literary romances in history was that of Sarah Helen Whitman and Edgar Allan Poe. Although Poe saw Whitman first, instantly becoming infatuated, it was a flirtatious valentine that *she* wrote to *him* that initiated their courtship. She had submitted the poem "To Edgar A. Poe" to a Valentine's Day party among the literati (which Poe was not invited to) in 1848. Due to the scandal and gossip surrounding Poe at the time, Whitman's valentine was not even read. In protest, Whitman had it published in *The Home Journal* the following month, making sure that Poe got to see it. At this point, she still had no idea that Poe had seen her outside her home three years earlier.

After seeing the flattering tribute, Poe returned the favor by tearing out a copy of his poem "To Helen" (which had been written for Jane Stanard but conveniently bore a nickname of Whitman's in the title) and sending it to her anonymously. Later, he sent her a poem written especially for her, which would become his second "To Helen." This poem recounts his first time seeing her, when she was in her rose garden on that moonlit summer night in July. In September 1848, Poe traveled to Providence for the second time and called on Whitman at her home on Benefit Street. This meeting went so well that Poe proposed to her right then and there! Whitman agreed to marry Poe on the condition that he abstain from alcohol. They planned to marry on Christmas Day, as long as Poe kept his promise.

Two days before the wedding, an anonymous note was delivered to Whitman claiming that Poe had had a glass of wine at his hotel. Whitman called off the wedding. Poe pleaded with her while she huffed an ether-soaked handkerchief (which she used to help her heart condition). Whitman then fainted on a couch, and Poe knelt by her side while holding her hand and begged her to say that she loved him. She said a final "I love you" to Poe before her mother kicked him out of the house. They never saw each other again. However, Whitman spent the next thirty years of her life defending Poe from the slanders being published about him. She corresponded with Poe's earliest biographers to ensure a fair handling of his legacy and even wrote her own biography, *Edgar Poe and His Critics* (more on that later)!

THE MORE YOU KNOW

Sarah Helen Whitman was also heavily involved in the Spiritualism movement, which was becoming quite popular around the time. She attended the very first recorded séance in Providence in 1850. As a practiced medium, she attempted to contact Edgar Allan Poe in the afterlife, and claimed that she was successful in doing so.

"Hopelessly Ill in Body and Mind"

Poe's infatuation with Annie Richmond overlapped his engagement to Sarah Helen Whitman. This became quite a hectic time for Poe, as he actively pursued both women. Poe wrote love letters to them just days apart. On November 14, Poe wrote to Whitman: "My own dearest Helen, so kind so true, so generous—so unmoved by all that would have moved one who had been less than angel . . . " Two days later, he wrote to Annie: "So long as I think that you know I love you, as no man ever loved woman—so long as I think you comprehend in some measure, the fervor with which I adore you, so long, no worldly trouble can ever render me absolutely wretched."

It was at this time that Poe attempted suicide by overdosing on laudanum, which was a concoction of alcohol and opium. Laudanum was widely used medicinally as a painkiller in the nineteenth century, but Poe's intentions with the drug were much darker. According to Poe, he acquired 2 ounces in Providence before boarding a train to Boston. He planned to take 1 ounce, then mail a letter to Annie that asked her to come to his side as he took the second ounce and ended his life. However, that first dose made him so sick that he couldn't complete the task. (It's unknown how much of this was fabricated on Poe's part to emphasize to his beloved Annie his emotional distress.)

Regardless, Poe described the ordeal in a letter written to Annie just over a week later. Near the end of his letter, he wrote: "I am so *ill—so* terribly, hopelessly ILL in body and mind, that I feel I CANNOT live, unless I can feel your sweet, gentle, loving hand pressed upon my forehead." This was among many instances in the last year of Poe's life where he foreshadowed his own untimely end.

THE MORE YOU KNOW

One of the many lies that Rufus Wilmot Griswold published about Poe after his death was that he was an opium addict. This is simply not true: Poe's only recorded dabbling with opium is this account, where he used it in an attempt on his own life. Many people contested Griswold's claim that Poe was a drug user, including Thomas Dunn English, the man Poe had a fistfight with over the letters scandal of 1846.

"Landor's Cottage"

Edgar Allan Poe's last completed work of prose was "Landor's Cottage," a tale composed completely of descriptions of a landscape's beauty and tranquility. Devoid of any horror, mystery, or madness, the story just consists of paragraphs about the serene nature that surrounds the narrator as he travels to an old Dutch cottage through the river valleys of New York. The story features themes from Poe's life, including the Dutch cottage itself, modeled after the one where he was living in Fordham, New York. Another element straight from Poe's own life was the character named Annie, after Nancy "Annie" Richmond.

In this tale, Poe describes the character Annie as a slender, beautiful, twenty-eight-year-old woman with light chestnut–colored hair. Her deep-set eyes are "spiritual gray" and her expression romantic. The story as a whole is thought to be a tribute to Annie, and even an ode to Poe's dream of moving into a cottage near her. He wrote in a letter to Annie in November 1848: "It is not *much* that I ask, *sweet sister Annie*—my mother & myself would take a small cottage at Westford—oh *so* small—so *very* humble—I should be far away from the tumult[s] of the world—from the ambition which I loathe—I would labor day & night, and with industry, I could accomplish *so* much—Annie! it would be a Paradise beyond my wildest hopes."

"A Pendant to 'The Domain of Arnheim,'" Poe's subtitle to "Landor's Cottage," refers to another one of Poe's more deeply sentimental works in the guise of a landscape piece. "Landor's Cottage" was published in Boston's *Flag of Our Union* magazine on June 9, 1849, just four months before his death.

LITERARY CONNECTIONS

While "Landor's Cottage" was Poe's last published work (and believed to be his last *completed* work), there was an incomplete, untitled manuscript among Poe's papers when he died. This unfinished story is framed as diary entries from a lighthouse keeper in the late eighteenth century. Scholars have given it their own title, "The Lighthouse." Today, fans still long to know what Poe planned for the plot of this story, but it is just another mystery that he took to his grave!

Appointing a Literary Executor

There is no documentation to prove it, but apparently, sometime in the early months of 1849, Poe informed his mother-in-law, Maria Clemm, that in the event of his death (which would occur that very year), he wished for Rufus Griswold to be his literary executor and Nathaniel Parker Willis (his former boss at the *Evening Mirror*) his biographer. She noted this in the preface she wrote for Griswold's editions of Poe's works. Clemm claimed that these wishes were written down somewhere by Poe himself, but they have never surfaced.

Scholars believe it's not entirely unlikely that Poe would have made these specific requests to his mother-in-law. While he harbored negative opinions of Griswold and Willis, he recognized that their literary success made them the right people to handle his literary estate and biography. It's thought that Clemm would have not likely known the specifics of these men's association with Poe if he hadn't talked about them with her. Whether it was actually his own wish or not, when Poe died, Clemm legally arranged for Griswold to be Poe's literary executor. It was by far the most damaging decision for Poe's legacy.

Griswold took complete control of everything related to Poe's life and works. It is unclear whether Willis was aware of Poe's purported wish to have him be his biographer, but he wrote some notices of Poe that were republished in a set of the two initial volumes of Griswold's *The Works of the Late Edgar Allan Poe*. Maria Clemm sent Griswold most of Poe's manuscripts, and volumes 1 and 2 of his works were compiled and published within a few months. These were supposed to financially benefit Clemm, who was alone and destitute after Poe's death. However, Griswold gave her only six sets of the volumes for her to sell however she could, and she saw none of the monetary compensation that Griswold had promised. In fact, the manuscripts she had given Griswold were worth far more than what she could have ever gotten from the sales of the volumes.

LITERARY CONNECTIONS

The set containing the initial two volumes of *The Works of the Late Edgar Allan Poe*, published by Rufus Wilmot Griswold, was just the beginning. Between 1849 and Griswold's death in 1857, he edited multiple editions of Poe's collected works. Eventually, Maria Clemm's foreword was replaced with Griswold's defamatory "memoir," which did irreversible damage to Poe's legacy. Biographers have since been sorting out fact from fiction when it comes to Poe's life.

More Than a Mother

According to Maria Clemm, when she made Rufus Griswold her son-in-law's literary executor, she was only doing what she thought was right (and if you take her word for it, what Poe had *requested* her to do). She was also trying to keep herself afloat, hoping that the sales of Poe's collected works would give her the money she desperately needed to survive now that she was completely alone. The bond that Clemm had with her son-in-law was like no other in his life.

That bond is exemplified in "To My Mother," a poem written for Clemm and published within the final months of Poe's life. Clemm would stay up through the night, rocking in her chair, as he wrote at his desk. She would prepare cup after cup of coffee at his request and listen to his ideas for new works. She was his devoted support system as well as his affectionate "Mother."

The sentiment expressed in the poem is poignant. Poe explains that Maria Clemm is dearer to his heart and more precious than his biological mother. He stresses that Clemm's importance as "Mother" comes primarily from being the mother of his wife, which made her "more than a mother" to him. She would go on to outlive her daughter and son-in-law by many years, passing away in 1871 at the age of eighty. Until her dying day, she relished the memory of her beloved "Eddy," as she and Virginia called him.

THE MORE YOU KNOW

Despite the warm, sweet, and tender representation of Maria Clemm by Poe in his sonnet, she was known by many people in their circle to be quite capricious and cold-hearted at times. She boarded with a number of Poe's friends and admirers after his death, accepting the charity of whoever was willing to take her in. However, she wore out her welcome on more than one occasion, often involving herself in household matters that didn't concern her. She ended up passing away in the same building as Poe, which, beginning in 1857, the Episcopal Church operated jointly as a hospital and long-term care facility. Her last request was to be buried next to her "Eddy," and she was.

"To My Mother"

Because I feel that, in the Heavens above,
The angels, whispering to one another,
Can find, among their burning terms of love,
None so devotional as that of "Mother,"
Therefore by that dear name I long have called you—
You who are more than mother unto me,
And fill my heart of hearts, where Death installed you
In setting my Virginia's spirit free.
My mother—my own mother, who died early,
Was but the mother of myself; but you
Are mother to the one I loved so dearly,
And thus are dearer than the mother I knew
By that infinity with which my wife
Was dearer to my soul than its soul-life.

Imprisoned, Pale, and Haggard

The final months of Edgar Allan Poe's life were filled with a slew of bizarre and unfortunate events—which eventually led to his bizarre and unfortunate death. Sometime in early July 1849, Poe was jailed at the Moyamensing Prison in Philadelphia, apparently for being drunk. According to a letter he wrote to Maria Clemm on July 7, he was imprisoned for only a few hours before he was recognized as "Poe, the poet" and released without a fine. His behavior after he was released was reported to be even more strange.

According to his friend John Sartain, a Philadelphia engraver, Poe called on him in the afternoon hours at his studio, which was located on the first floor of his home. He described Poe as "pale and haggard," with a "wild and frightened" look in his eyes. Poe explained to Sartain that he was seeking protection after he overheard some men on the train plotting to kill him. When Sartain asked why anyone would want to kill him, Poe replied that it was over a woman. Poe asked his friend to borrow a razor so that he could shave off his mustache, thinking that he would be less recognizable. Sartain was so concerned about Poe's mental state that instead of giving Poe a razor for fear Poe would hurt himself, he went ahead and cut off Poe's mustache using a pair of scissors. Sartain assured Poe that he would be safe with him.

Later that evening, Sartain took Poe for a walk to the Fairmount Water Works, which overlooked the Schuylkill River. Sartain made sure to stay between Poe and the river, for fear that Poe was going to throw himself in it. During their walk, Poe told Sartain about his imprisonment and said that while in prison, he had a hallucination of his mother-in-law, Maria Clemm, being dismembered, which caused him to start convulsing. Sartain took Poe back to his house and made him a bed on the sofa. Stretched out on three chairs, Sartain slept by his side. Apparently, Poe recovered and left within a few days.

THE MORE YOU KNOW

If John Sartain's account is accurate, Poe's behavior (the fact that he thought men were out to kill him and he was having delusions and hallucinations) could explain that a serious mental health condition might have contributed to his death only months later. Sartain was evidently concerned that Poe was going to hurt himself, and Poe's attempted laudanum overdose has led to speculation that he had suicidal thoughts. Additionally, just days before he died, Poe was found delirious and wearing clothes that didn't appear to belong to him. Scholars and fans alike still wonder: Was Poe trying to disguise himself, like he was in Sartain's account? Was he suffering from paranoid delusions? Were there really men plotting to kill him? These are just a few of the strange pieces to the bizarre puzzle that was the end of Poe's life.

"No Desire to Live"

Not only was Edgar Allan Poe experiencing confounding mental and physical health crises in the months leading up to his death, but he was also claiming that death could be his only respite. Shortly after his imprisonment and the frightening encounter with John Sartain, Poe wrote to Maria Clemm, "The very instant you get this, *come* to me. The joy of seeing you will almost compensate for our sorrows. We can but die together. It *is* no use to reason with me *now*; I must die. I have no desire to live since I have done 'Eureka.' I could accomplish nothing more. For your sake it would be sweet to live, but we must die together. You have been all in all to me, darling, ever beloved mother, and dearest, truest friend. I was never *really* insane, except on occasions where my heart was touched."

In the same letter, Poe told Clemm that he had been ill from cholera, which caused him spasms that left him unable to even hold a pen. When Poe would have a drinking binge while away from his mother-in-law, he would often tell her that the reason for his delay in writing to her was that he was "ill" so she wouldn't worry about his drinking.

At the time of this letter, Poe had been away from his mother-in-law for months and was terribly homesick. He said that he could bear anything when he was with her, but when he was away from her, he was too miserable to even live. In another letter, Poe wrote, "Oh God, my Mother, shall we ever again meet? If possible, oh come! My clothes are *so horrible,* and I am *so ill.* Oh, if you *could* come to me, *my mother.* Write instantly—oh *do* not fail. God forever bless you." But they didn't meet again: Poe died before he could return to her.

THE MORE YOU KNOW

Among the letters that Poe wrote to Maria Clemm in the summer of 1849 was one informing her that his suitcase had been lost for ten days. Upon finding it at the depot in Philadelphia, he discovered that copies of both the lectures he was scheduled to deliver had been stolen. He had to quickly rewrite at least one of them.

The First and Last Fiancée

Edgar Allan Poe's lecture tour brought him back to his hometown of Richmond, Virginia, in the summer of 1849. It was then and there that he rekindled his romance with his first fiancée, the now widowed Sarah Elmira Royster Shelton, after calling on her at her home. She recalled, "That very morning I told him I was going to church that I never let anything interfere with that, that he must call again and when he did call again he renewed his addresses. I laughed at it, he looked very serious and said he was in earnest. . . . I told him if he would not take a positive denial he must give me time to consider of it—and he said a love that hesitated was not a love for him."

While Elmira was dismissive of Poe at first, he quickly won her over. The two became engaged for the second time (over twenty years after their first engagement!), and this time, things were looking promising. Elmira's late husband had left her property in the amount of $60,000 as long as she remained his widow, but if she were to marry Poe, she would retain only a house, furniture, servants, a carriage, and an income of about $1,400. Still, the reduced income would be more than enough for them to live a very comfortable life, even including Maria Clemm in the household.

In one of the last letters Poe wrote to Maria Clemm, he told her, "I confess that my heart sinks at the idea of this marriage. *I think*, however, that it will certainly take place & that immediately." Poe had his doubts that the marriage would happen, given his prior experience with his engagement to Sarah Helen Whitman. Like Whitman, Elmira asked Poe to remain sober, which, once again, he agreed to. This time, he would take the promise a step further to prove his intentions.

--------- **THE MORE YOU KNOW** ---------

After Poe's death, Sarah Elmira Royster Shelton hardly acknowledged having ties with him. Her children despised Poe, wishing that their mother had never even entertained the idea of marrying him. So, Elmira, mostly out of respect for her adult children, disavowed her association with Poe. She refused any interviews about her relationship with him until 1875, when she granted a Poe admirer, Edward V. Valentine, a brief interview. While she shared some minor details about her relationship with Poe, she denied that she was engaged to him when he died.

Temperance Pledge

Edgar Allan Poe's issue with alcohol has become inextricably bound up with his image in the popular mind. The slander published during and after his lifetime only caricaturized the issue. Alcohol was a vice he was quite aware of, and he made many promises throughout his life to refrain from drinking. Poe's troublesome relationship with alcohol was seen by society at that time as a character flaw and not an addiction. It was believed to exhibit a lack of self-control, which was deemed weak and immoral. Today, much of what people think they know about Poe's alcohol use is hyperbole and fabrication. Based on Poe's literary output alone, scholars have determined that there was no way he was intoxicated *all* of the time or even *a lot* of the time. In fact, Poe was sober *most* of the time. His bouts with alcohol were few and far between, and he didn't have to drink to excess to become drunk. As previously discussed, friends witnessed him drink no more than a single glass of wine before he became completely inebriated, and then it would take him days to recover. Given the descriptions of Poe's drinking sprees, some scholars suggest that he had an intolerance or allergy to alcohol.

In the summer of 1849, Poe decided once and for all to abstain from the bottle. Around this time, Poe apparently had a bout with liquor that nearly killed him. He was told by two physicians that another binge would be fatal. The pledge would also help him win Elmira's hand for a second engagement.

Poe became a member of the Shockoe Hill Division, No. 54, of the Sons of Temperance in Richmond, signing his name to an oath that he took with what was described as "unusual firmness," as if "impatient for the opportunity." One friend reported that during Poe's time in Philadelphia, he went almost two years without a drop of alcohol; Poe believed he could fulfill his pledge. Unfortunately, he died just months later, and there is still a question of whether alcohol played a role in his death.

LITERARY CONNECTIONS

Edgar Allan Poe's short story "The Angel of the Odd" was published in October 1844 in the *Columbian Lady's and Gentleman's Magazine*. This was way before Poe joined the Sons of Temperance; however, some believe the story includes a message about abstaining from alcohol. The narrator drinks himself to sleep after being visited by a bizarre figure composed of a keg and wine bottles, which presents itself as the "angel of the odd." A series of unfortunate events for the narrator follows this alcohol-induced slumber. The angel reappears, forcing the narrator to admit that strange things do happen. Only then do things return to normal for him.

"Annabel Lee"

Edgar Allan Poe's "Annabel Lee" is a masterpiece of gothic romanticism. The poem delves into Poe's usual themes of love, loss, and grief, describing a childhood love that transcends time and even death. It is arguably one of Poe's most famous poems, next to "The Raven." Poe submitted the poem to be published alongside his wedding announcement to Elmira. Instead, "Annabel Lee" was published alongside his obituary. Scholars accept it as the last poem Poe ever wrote.

While Elmira is a likely candidate, practically every woman who ever knew Poe claimed to be his Annabel Lee. Elmira is a candidate because she and Poe were young and in love before her "highborn kinsman came" (her father) "and bore her away." But another contender is Sarah Helen Whitman, who believed that she was the subject of the poem. Annie Richmond, yet another possibility, was promised a copy of the poem by Poe around May 1849. A number of other women have also claimed the poem was written about them.

Then there is Virginia Clemm Poe, Poe's wife. Frances Osgood, who was very close with both Poe and Virginia, claimed that "Annabel Lee" was in fact written for Virginia. Some believe this would make a lot of sense, since

Poe and Virginia met when she was very young and they married young. The "wind that blew out of the cloud" that killed Annabel Lee could be a metaphor for tuberculosis, the disease that took Virginia from Poe. Others theorize that the poem was written with no particular woman in mind or that Annabel Lee was an amalgam of all the women Poe loved and lost. Whatever the inspiration for the poem, it continues to be a fan favorite today.

LITERARY CONNECTIONS

The main reason why Sarah Helen Whitman believed that she was Poe's Annabel Lee was a poem she wrote shortly after their breakup, published in February 1849. The poem, which was initially titled "Stanzas for Music," then retitled "Our Island of Dreams," contains lines like "Tell him I lingered alone on the shore," "The night wind blew cold on my desolate heart," and "When the clouds that now veil from us Heaven's fair light." Whitman believed that Poe's lines in "Annabel Lee" echoed hers, which prompted her to think that "Annabel Lee" was written in response to her poem (which came first) and therefore was about her.

Opening Lines of "Annabel Lee"

It was many and many a year ago,
In a kingdom by the sea,
That a maiden there lived whom you may know
By the name of Annabel Lee;
And this maiden she lived with no other thought
Than to love and be loved by me.

I was a child and *she* was a child,
In this kingdom by the sea,
But we loved with a love that was more than love—
I and my Annabel Lee—
With a love that the wingèd seraphs of Heaven
Coveted her and me.

And this was the reason that, long ago,
In this kingdom by the sea,
A wind blew out of a cloud, chilling
My beautiful Annabel Lee;
So that her highborn kinsmen came
And bore her away from me,
To shut her up in a sepulchre
In this kingdom by the sea.

The angels, not half so happy in Heaven,
Went envying her and me—
Yes!—that was the reason (as all men know,
In this kingdom by the sea)
That the wind came out of the cloud by night,
Chilling and killing my Annabel Lee.

Final Journey

O n September 24, 1849, Edgar Allan Poe gave his final lecture on "The Poetic Principal" at the Exchange Hotel in Richmond. His ambitious plan from that point on was to leave for Baltimore via steamboat early Thursday morning, September 27. He planned to take the train north from Baltimore to Philadelphia, where he would conduct some business before traveling to New York. There, he would pick up Maria Clemm and take her to Richmond to witness his marriage to Elmira and then to live with the couple. However, this journey didn't go according to plan.

LITERARY CONNECTIONS

The "business" awaiting Poe in Philadelphia was a lucky one. Commissioned by a wealthy piano manufacturer, who was the husband of minor poet Marguerite St. Leon Loud, to edit his wife's debut poetry collection, Poe had the opportunity to earn a quick and substantial sum of $100. He estimated the task would take no more than three days. But due to his sudden death, he never got to edit that collection, titled *Wayside Flowers*, which was published in Boston in 1851.

On the evening of September 26, Poe visited Elmira to say his goodbyes. However, she noticed that he was very sad, and he complained that he didn't feel well. Elmira checked his pulse and felt his forehead, noticing he had a fever. She advised him not to travel. To ease Elmira's worries, some think Poe may have promised her that he would see his friend, a physician named John Carter, before his departure. Around nine thirty, he visited Carter at his office. The visit was more social than medical. While the two chatted, Poe was fiddling with Carter's Malacca sword-cane before deciding to get a late dinner at Sadler's Restaurant nearby. Oddly, Poe took Carter's sword-cane with him and left his own walking stick behind. (It would be hard to mistake the two, as Carter's cane was much heavier than Poe's walking stick.)

Around midnight, Poe left Sadler's Restaurant, headed for one of the early morning steamboats bound for Baltimore. Sadler claimed that Poe left the restaurant in good spirits and was sober. Before he boarded the steamboat, Poe apparently stopped by the Mackenzie household (where his sister lived with her adopted family), because they ended up with Carter's cane. In the early morning hours of September 27, Poe left Richmond without his trunk, which he left in his room at the Swan Tavern. After a restless night, Elmira went to check on Poe and was reportedly devastated to find that he had left Richmond despite not having felt well just hours before. Poe's whereabouts wouldn't be known for nearly a week, when he was found near death in Baltimore on October 3.

"Rather the Worse for Wear"

On October 3, 1849, in Baltimore, Maryland, a newspaper compositor named Joseph W. Walker stumbled on an incoherent man at Gunner's Hall tavern. The man was sitting drooped forward in an armchair with his unkempt hair falling over his broad forehead. He looked haggard and was dressed in dingy, ill-fitting clothes. The unfortunate man was Edgar Allan Poe, and this was the first recorded appearance of Poe since leaving Richmond on September 27.

Poe was able to tell Walker his name and say that he knew a resident of the city, Joseph Evans Snodgrass. Walker immediately wrote the following note to Snodgrass:

> Dear Sir,—
>
> There is a gentleman, rather the worse for wear, at Ryan's 4th ward polls, who goes under the cognomen of Edgar A. Poe, and who appears in great distress, & he says he is acquainted with you, and I assure you, he is need of immediate assistance,
>
> Yours, in haste,
> Jos. W. Walker

When Snodgrass arrived at the tavern, he recognized Poe. With the help of a waiter, he brought Poe to one of the upstairs rooms where he could be more comfortable until relatives could be notified.

THE MORE YOU KNOW

It was a local election day when Poe was found at Gunner's Hall, which was also being used as a polling place. This has led to the theory that Poe was a victim of "cooping," a political practice of the time where ruffians were hired to kidnap people and ply them with alcohol to manipulate them to vote multiple times for their candidate. They would even swap out different articles of clothing to dupe voting officials (who knew exactly what was going on and turned a blind eye to it). This could explain why Poe was wearing clothes that appeared not to belong to him and why he was delirious when Walker found him.

Poe's uncle through marriage, Henry Herring, arrived and decided to have Poe brought to the nearby Washington College Hospital rather than to his house. Herring claimed that "[Poe] so frequently abused his hospitality by the rudeness as well as vulgarity of his bearing while drunk, toward the ladies of his household [that he] couldn't think, for a moment, of taking him to his house in his present besotted condition."

So, Poe was carried to a carriage waiting outside. Onlookers watched as Poe's body was placed in the carriage and sent on its way unattended. Herring didn't even pay the fare, and Poe wouldn't live to pay it himself.

"Lord Help My Poor Soul"

When Edgar Allan Poe arrived at the Washington College Hospital around five o'clock in the evening, he was unable to speak coherently and seemed unaware of the condition he was in. Hospital staff removed him from the carriage and brought him to the public ward, assuming that he was a drunken charity case. Poe couldn't advocate for himself, and because nobody accompanied him to the hospital, the staff had no idea who he was or the circumstances of his arrival. It was not until later that they learned the famous poet was in their care, and they gave him a private room. Poe's care was overseen by the attending physician, Dr. John J. Moran. (Because Moran was overseeing the entire hospital, many are skeptical that he dedicated as much time to Poe as he would claim.)

Hearing the news of his cousin's admittance to the hospital, Neilson Poe (who Edgar considered one of his greatest enemies) went to check on him on October 4. Moran didn't permit any visitors and turned Neilson away. The following day (October 5), Neilson sent a clean change of linens, and this time he was told that Poe was doing much better . . . only to hear of his cousin's death two days later.

Over the four days Poe spent in the hospital, he slipped in and out of consciousness, never able to say what exactly happened to him. He was described as being pale, drenched in sweat, and often muttering without making the slightest sense. He imagined seeing objects on the walls and would alternate between violent, excitable fits and periods of utter calm. He was able to tell Moran that he had a wife in Richmond (likely referring to Elmira, who was technically not yet his wife). He also told Moran at some point that he was ready to "sink in the earth." On the evening of October 6, Poe repeatedly called out the name "Reynolds" until around five o'clock the next morning, Sunday, October 7. Finally, he became quiet. Gently swaying his head from side to side while nurses pressed cold compresses to his head, Edgar Allan Poe spoke his final words, "Lord help my poor soul," and died.

THE MORE YOU KNOW

One of the most puzzling mysteries of Poe's final days is his calling for "Reynolds" prior to his death. Some believe Poe was referring to Henry R. Reynolds, one of the election officials at the polling place where Poe had been found just days before. Others believe that Reynolds refers to the author of the "Address on the Subject of a Surveying and Exploring Expedition to the Pacific Ocean and South Seas," which was thought to have given Poe ideas for his only novel, *The Narrative of Arthur Gordon Pym of Nantucket*.

"Buried Like a Dog"

After Poe's death, his cousin, Neilson Poe, and uncle, Henry Herring, began making arrangements for his funeral. His uncle was a lumber dealer, so he pulled some "neat" mahogany from his supply and sent it to a local cabinet maker to furnish Poe's coffin. The coffin lacked any lining, handles, a nameplate, or even a cushion for the poet's corpse to rest his weary head. Poe's all-black burial clothes were apparently donated by the students of the medical college where he died, and Moran himself supplied a white cravat and collar. Moran's wife sewed the burial shroud.

Poe's body was prepared in the hospital, and in the early morning and afternoon of October 8, his body lay in state in the rotunda for people to pay their respects. Some of the city's prominent, wealthy women apparently visited Poe's remains to cut locks of his hair as a memento. Around four o'clock, the hackney provided by Neilson took Poe's remains from the hospital to the Westminster Burying Ground less than 2 miles away. Only seven people witnessed the funeral, including Poe's uncle Henry, cousin Neilson, Snodgrass, an old friend and classmate named Zaccheus Collins Lee, and the Reverend W.T.D. Clemm (a relative of Poe's wife), along with two gravediggers. Poor Maria Clemm and Elmira didn't hear the news of Poe's death until he was already in the ground.

It was a chilly, wet, dreadful afternoon as Edgar Allan Poe's remains were taken from the hackney to the freshly dug grave that awaited him in the back of the cemetery. The plot belonged to his grandfather, David Poe Sr., and contained the graves of both his grandparents and of his brother. Due to the weather and the few people in attendance, Reverend Clemm skipped the eulogy and simply read off the few lines necessary for the service. One onlooker who happened to pass by the cemetery noted that the service was "cold-blooded and unchristianlike." Poe's coffin was lowered directly into the ground without even a simple lining to protect it from the wet earth. After the funeral, the newspapers (local first, then national) started circulating a story that Poe was buried "like a dog." This wasn't far from the truth. The tragic end to the tragic life of the brilliant writer Edgar Allan Poe.

THE MORE YOU KNOW

Baltimore gave Edgar Allan Poe a proper send-off in 2009. Jeff Jerome, the curator of the Edgar Allan Poe House and Museum at the time, organized an elaborate wake and funeral for Poe. A body created by a local artist in Poe's likeness lay in state at the Poe House the Saturday night before the funeral procession. The following day, an antique horse-drawn carriage transported "Poe" from the house on Amity Street to the Westminster Hall, where an elaborate service was held. Over 700 people paid their respects to Poe that day, 160 years after Poe's actual funeral in 1849.

Edgar Allan Poe Is Dead

"**E**DGAR ALLAN POE is dead. He died in Baltimore the day before yesterday. This announcement will startle many, but few will be grieved by it" began the venomous obituary published in the *New-York Daily Tribune* on October 9, 1849. It was just two days since Poe had passed. The column was signed "Ludwig," the pseudonym of Poe's literary frenemy, Rufus Griswold. After Poe's death, Griswold was entrusted to be his literary executor and took the opportunity to also become his first biographer.

The obituary went on to describe Poe as a pitiful, friendless, melancholy madman that muttered to himself in the streets while dwelling in realms beyond this world. That characterization was simply not true, but it served as a precursor to the much longer biographical account that Griswold included in his edited volumes of Poe's works, where he elaborated on such lies and concocted even more. The slanders perpetuated by Griswold immediately following Poe's death created the myth of the famed author that many readers still believe to this day. In reality, Poe was a pretty normal person. He was human, and because he was human, he *was* flawed, but not to the extent that his defamer made him out to be.

Griswold's attempt to blot Poe's name out of existence by smearing his character ended up achieving just the opposite. In an unlikely twist of fate, Griswold made Poe *more* famous by handling his biography in a controversial manner—the same way that Poe handled his own fictional stories! A phenomenal posthumous comeback would vindicate Poe and ultimately prove him right. Edgar Allan Poe remains one of the most popular figures in literature today, while Rufus Griswold lies in an unmarked grave.

LITERARY CONNECTIONS

The final line in Rufus Wilmot Griswold's obituary for Poe was taken from *Macbeth*: "After life's fitful fever he sleeps well." It was an ironic choice, given the cruelty of the obituary. While Griswold did emphasize Poe's literary genius, he completely tarnished his personal character.

Dr. Moran

Scholars agree that one of the most frustrating aspects of Edgar Allan Poe's mysterious death is that the one man who *could* have provided the most telling details about it decided instead to exploit his connection to the famous poet's final days. Dr. John Moran is responsible for muddying the facts and even concocting lies about what happened between him and Poe up until Poe died. The letter Moran wrote to Maria Clemm in reply to her inquiries is thought to have the most accurate information, because it was written only five weeks after Poe's death, before Moran decided to cash in.

Moran was only in his twenties when he worked as the resident physician at what was known at the time as the Washington College Hospital. Since Moran was overseeing the entire facility, there's doubt that he personally attended to Poe very often, if at all. In fact, a Dr. William M. Cullen, who was serving his apprenticeship at the hospital at the time, claimed that it was he, not Moran, who provided care for Poe.

Moran went on to publish books and articles and even give lectures about his brief encounter as the physician who attended to Edgar Allan Poe's final days and subsequent death. Many times, Moran contradicted his own statements, which has helped scholars weed out the more obvious lies. A prime example is Moran's account of Poe's final words. In his letter to Maria Clemm, Moran tells her that Poe's last words were "Lord help my poor soul." Simple, and quite possible. Dr. Moran's recollections of Poe's last words became more dramatic over time. By 1875, they were "Self-murderer, there is a gulf beyond the stream Where is the buoy, lifeboat, ship of fire, sea of brass. Test, shore no more!" Finally, in 1885, he claimed Poe said, "He who arched the heavens and upholds the universe, has His decrees legibly written upon the frontlet of every human being, and upon demons incarnate."

LITERARY CONNECTIONS

In 1885, Dr. John J. Moran published his book about the death of Edgar Allan Poe. *A Defense of Edgar Allan Poe*, which he dedicated to Sarah Elmira Shelton. Shelton had granted Moran an interview where she admitted for the first time since Poe's death that she was in fact engaged to him when he died. Dr. Moran was already spreading misinformation about Poe's last days before this book was published. Scholars agree that the details Moran provides should all be taken with a grain of salt, if not challenged.

Cause(s) of Death

The exact cause of Edgar Allan Poe's death has been widely speculated about since 1849. Unfortunately, there are no known records from the hospital regarding Poe's case, not even a death certificate. Dr. Moran's oral account was that Poe died from phrenitis, or congestion of the brain, which is a broad term that doesn't accurately identify a cause. This was usually the diagnosis when a patient died from an unknown cause with symptoms of delirium, as in Poe's case.

The first question is whether alcohol played a role in Poe's death. Snodgrass (who came to Poe's aid at Gunner's Hall) was adamant that Poe was under the influence of alcohol when he was found. However, Snodgrass was a staunch member of the temperance movement and he used Poe's case as an example of the dangers of alcohol, which has led some to believe that his opinion was biased. Those who knew Poe *assumed* that alcohol played a role, since his symptoms resembled those when he was intoxicated. So, sadly, whatever serious health condition he was suffering from was likely ignored for that reason. Historically, it's known how alcohol affected Poe's mental and physical state, so it is likely that it did contribute to some degree to his condition when he was found. At the same time, Dr. Moran claimed that Poe didn't have the faintest hint of alcohol on his breath when he tended to Poe when Poe was admitted to the hospital. However, since Moran is known to have embellished the truth around his experience with Poe, his claims can't be taken as fact. This has created quite the conundrum for scholars trying to figure out what really happened to Edgar Allan Poe.

Some theories include cooping, mugging, bipolar disorder, suicide, heart disease, brain tumor, epilepsy, tuberculosis, meningitis, murder, rabies, pneumonia, carbon monoxide poisoning, cholera, alcohol poisoning/withdrawal/dehydrogenase, apoplexy, diabetes, and a drug overdose.

LITERARY CONNECTIONS

The rabies theory has been adopted as a popular explanation of Poe's death. However, it is based on the questionable recollections of Dr. John J. Moran. The theory was first published in the September 1996 issue of *Maryland Medical Journal* by cardiologist Dr. R. Michael Benitez. Dr. Benitez suggested rabies as the cause of death based on an account by Dr. Moran that Poe had difficulty swallowing liquids. But in other accounts, Dr. Moran stated that Poe drank fluids without difficulty.

It will likely never be known exactly what took Poe's life that fateful October day or why he was in such a bizarre condition in the days prior to his death. Some believe the safest scenario to bet on is that a combination of factors caused Edgar Allan Poe's death.

Poe Abroad

There's no question that Edgar Allan Poe is one of the most influential writers ever to come from the United States of America. Not only was his work widely read during his lifetime, but it also continues to be read almost two hundred years later. Poe's works are included in middle school, high school, and college curricula. But his influence doesn't stop there. Poe's works have been translated into languages all over the world, so readers from every corner of the globe can be haunted by the prolific works of the Master of the Macabre.

French, German, Spanish, Portuguese, Romanian, Russian, Korean, and Japanese are just some of the languages that Poe's works have been translated into. Poe's poetry and prose were beginning to be translated even in his lifetime. As early as 1846, his works were starting to be translated into German, Spanish, and French. After Poe's death in 1849, even more interest in the author was sparked, which caused more of Poe's works to be translated. Perhaps one of the most famous Poe translators is Charles Baudelaire, the French poet and essayist who became Poe's European champion.

Baudelaire was responsible for bringing much attention to Poe in France. So much so that the public started to claim that French readers appreciated Poe before American readers did. In 1848, during Poe's lifetime, Baudelaire translated his first of Poe's stories, "Mesmeric Revelation." After Poe's death, Baudelaire followed up with more extensive translations of Poe's works, which were compiled in two volumes, *Histoires extraordinaires*, published in 1856, and *Nouvelles histoires extraordinaires*, published in 1857. Baudelaire also wrote several essays that highlighted the genius of Poe's literary output. The fact that Edgar Allan Poe's works have been translated so extensively is a true testament to the power of his writing and the interest it has captured across the world.

——— LITERARY CONNECTIONS ———

In 1875, the French poet Stéphane Mallarmé published his translation of "The Raven," accompanied with illustrations by the French artist Édouard Manet. Mallarmé sent a copy of "Le Corbeau" ("The Raven") to Poe's former fiancée, Sarah Helen Whitman. Whitman was fluent in multiple languages (including French), and Mallarmé sought her approval for translations of Poe's works that he would publish in the future. Manet's illustrations for "Le Corbeau" are among the most recognizable pieces of art associated with Poe's raven. The Providence Athenaeum owns an original bookplate featuring Manet's depiction of the raven, which was inscribed to Whitman by Mallarmé himself.

Edgar Poe and His Critics

While Edgar Allan Poe's works enjoyed international acclaim, his reputation still faced a concerted attack by Rufus Griswold. This prompted a vigorous defense of his character from a growing circle of admirers. One of the first was from Sarah Helen Whitman, a poet, an essayist, and a literary critic herself, though perhaps her most important connection to Poe was her brief engagement to him. Despite the tumultuous end to their relationship, Whitman became one of Poe's staunchest defenders.

In 1860, Whitman published a brief book, *Edgar Poe and His Critics*, which served as both a mini biography and a defense of his legacy. In her preface, Whitman directly addresses Griswold: "DR. GRISWOLD's Memoir of Edgar Poe has been extensively read and circulated; its perverted facts and baseless assumptions have been adopted into every subsequent memoir and notice of the poet, and have been translated into many languages. For ten years this great wrong to the dead has passed unchallenged and unrebuked. It has been assumed by a recent English critic that 'Edgar Poe had no friends.' As an index to a more equitable and intelligible theory of the idiosyncrasies of his life, and as an earnest protest against the spirit of Dr. Griswold's unjust memoir, these pages are submitted to his more candid readers and critics by ONE OF HIS FRIENDS."

While it's believed that Whitman waited to publish her book until after Griswold's death to avoid any backlash from him, its publication is still seen as a brave act. It was not exactly convenient for anyone in literary circles to challenge Rufus Griswold's work (even after his death). But Whitman, having known Poe quite intimately, was aware of the injustice done to him by Griswold. Whitman also assisted several Poe biographers in writing their own works. Two of them were among the foremost Poe biographers at the time: John Henry Ingram and William F. Gill.

LITERARY CONNECTIONS

Sarah "Sallie" Robins, a resident of Putnam, Ohio, aspired to write her own Poe biography after reading Sarah Helen Whitman's *Edgar Poe and His Critics*. In 1860, she contacted Whitman, who shared her materials, including a daguerreotype of Poe and an edition of her own poetry collection, titled *Hours of Life, and Other Poems*. Robins also invited Poe's mother-in-law, Maria Clemm, to live in her home to aid her research. Clemm did move in; however, Robins was institutionalized in 1862 for an unknown reason and remained there until 1868. The year following her return home, she passed away at thirty-two years old, leaving her Poe biography unfinished.

Battling Biographers

Several would-be biographers stepped up to challenge Rufus Griswold's venomous memoir of Poe and correct the lies that were being published about him. One of those who took up the challenge was John Henry Ingram, an aspiring poet who early in his life first became aware of Poe. Ingram was an Englishman raised in Stoke Newington, the same town where Poe spent his early years with his foster parents. He began publishing articles on Poe's life and works in the early 1870s, when Poe had gained international attention. In 1874, he published his memoir of Poe in an attempt to erase Griswold's defamatory one. But others were setting out to do the same, which brought out a competitive side of Ingram that showed he could be capricious and petty (more on this later).

William F. Gill was an American writer and editor best known for his 1877 biography, *The Life of Edgar Allan Poe*, which served as another crucial narrative countering Griswold's malicious and inaccurate one. Seeking to restore Poe's image, Gill diligently researched Poe's life, corresponding with his associates to gather firsthand accounts and correct the historical record. This was happening at precisely the same time that Ingram was writing his biography. Nancy "Annie" Richmond, Marie Louise Shew, and Sarah Helen

Whitman were among the few people still alive who knew Poe, and they served as sources for information about him. The problem was, the women were giving both Ingram and Gill similar information, which made their works appear unoriginal when published.

Ingram and Gill each published articles that disputed the other's sources, claiming that the other copied material from him. And in trying to write their defenses of Poe, they actually discredited each other's work with their accusations. Ingram's four-volume set, published in monthly installments between 1874 and 1875, came before Gill's 1877 biography. Ingram's and Gill's imaginations and their hasty, competitive writing resulted in biographies filled with inaccuracies. Despite their books becoming some of the most widely read biographies of Poe in the late nineteenth century (Ingram's was even reprinted several times), there was still much more work to be done to set the record straight!

───────── LITERARY CONNECTIONS ─────────

In addition to John Henry Ingram and William F. Gill, there were two other foremost nineteenth-century biographers of Poe: Richard Henry Stoddard and Eugene L. Didier. The turn of the twentieth century brought new biographers and editors of Poe's works, who have all solidified their place in Poe scholarship. A few of these are Mary E. Phillips, Hervey Allen, Arthur Hobson Quinn, and Thomas Ollive Mabbott.

Pennies for Poe

With the surge of interest in Edgar Allan Poe's life and works after his death, the public started to wonder about Poe's remains. In 1860, Poe's cousin Neilson commissioned a modest marble headstone after Maria Clemm wrote to him in concern for her dear "Eddy's" unmarked grave, which was overgrown with weeds. However, the stone Neilson commissioned from the carver, Hugh Sisson, was destroyed when a train derailed from the tracks near the shop, barreling through Sisson's monument yard and causing a substantial amount of damage, including the destruction of Poe's headstone. Neilson didn't pay for another headstone after this.

So, Poe, lying in an unmarked grave for sixteen years, seemed destined to lack a marker for his burial spot—until a Baltimore schoolteacher named Sara Sigourney Rice began raising funds to erect a worthy monument to the famed American writer. Her campaign started in 1865, and by 1871, she had raised about half the funds necessary for a marble monument from private donations, benefits, and pennies donated by Baltimore schoolchildren. In 1874, a Philadelphia philanthropist named George W. Childs donated the remainder. The total cost was a little over $1,500 (over $40,000 today).

The grand marble structure, standing on a granite base and reaching a height of over 7 feet, was designed by George

A. Frederick, the architect who designed the Baltimore City Hall, and constructed by Hugh Sisson (the man hired to build Poe's initial headstone). A portrait of Poe in bronze relief adorns the front of the monument, and his full name appears in large letters along the bottom. The monument was unveiled before a large crowd on November 17, 1875, in the northwest corner of the Westminster Burying Ground, near the entry gates. However, Poe had been buried in his grandfather's lot in the *back* of the cemetery, so how did he come to lie under the monument in the front? Well, two exhumations and three burials later.

LITERARY CONNECTIONS

One notable attendee of Poe's monument dedication was the poet Walt Whitman, who later said of Poe and the ceremony: "I have felt a strong impulse to come over and be here to-day myself in memory of Poe, which I have obey'd, but not the slightest impulse to make a speech, which, my dear friends, must also be obeyed." He also stated, "For a long while, and until lately, I had a distaste for Poe's writings. I wanted, and still want for poetry, the clear sun shining, and fresh air blowing—the strength and power of health, not of delirium, even amid the stormiest passions—with always the background of the eternal moralities. Non-complying with these requirements, Poe's genius has yet conquer'd a special recognition for itself, and I too have come to fully admit it, and appreciate it and him."

Three Graves

Once the monument was finished there was the matter of where to put it. Originally, the monument committee suggested placing it in the northwest corner of the burial grounds, near the front gates. That way, tourists could see the monument at any time, whether the gates were locked or not. However, Poe's cousin Neilson requested that Poe's remains be undisturbed. So, it was decided to erect the monument over Poe's remains where they were in the back of the cemetery, behind the church. However, this posed a problem: The location of Poe's grave in the Poe family plot left no room to erect the monument, as it would interfere with neighboring graves.

Poe's remains would have to be disturbed after all, and placed with Maria Clemm's about 12 feet away from Poe's in a less crowded area of the graveyard. The exhumation took place on September 30, 1875. After the gravediggers dug about 5 feet down, they reached the coffin of Edgar Allan Poe. Inside was an almost perfect skeleton, with the hands resting one over the other and some hair clinging to the forehead. Poe's teeth were described as perfect, the top row having fallen out of the skull, while the bottom row was still attached to the lower jaw. The coffin and remains were placed in a wooden case and reinterred in their new location. The monument was erected above the new grave the following day.

As people heard about the magnificent gravestone erected for Poe, they visited the graveyard only to find that it was hidden behind the church. When the gates were locked, there was no way to see the monument at all. Pressure from the public forced the monument committee to revisit their original plan, and a second exhumation took place on November 5, five weeks after the first. George W. Spence, the sexton of the church and burial ground, officiated at all three burials and both exhumations of Poe, from 1849 to 1875. Poe's and Maria Clemm's remains were relocated to the northwest corner of the graveyard. The monument followed soon after, and the dedication took place. Meanwhile, Virginia Poe was hundreds of miles away in Fordham, New York. Her remains would join her husband's and mother's—after their own journey.

THE MORE YOU KNOW

A Baltimore philanthropist named Orrin C. Painter had Poe's original grave marked with a stone of its own in October 1912. The stone reads: "Original burial place of Edgar Allan Poe from October 9, 1849, until November 17, 1875. Mrs. Maria Clemm, his mother-in-law, lies upon his right, and Virginia Poe, his wife, upon his left, under the monument erected to him in this cemetery." Today, when you visit the Westminster Burying Ground, you can visit both burial locations of Edgar Allan Poe.

Virginia's Bones

Over in New York, Virginia Poe's remains were in a cemetery in Fordham, having been interred in the family vault of John Valentine, the landlord from whom they rented the quaint farm cottage where Virginia died in 1847. In 1883, the cemetery was being razed, with multiple remains exhumed, and disposed of if unclaimed. Virginia's bones nearly fell victim to this ignoble removal, to be lost to history!

Tradition has it that William Gill, one of the foremost Poe biographers at the time, got to the cemetery right as the sexton had Virginia's unclaimed remains in his shovel, ready to be tossed into a mass grave. Gill collected them, put them in a small box, took them home, and corresponded with Neilson Poe in Baltimore to get them placed next to the remains of her husband and mother. Gill kept the remains under his bed for two years, often showing them off as the remains of "Annabel Lee" to his houseguests. Despite this strange handling of Virginia's remains, Gill has gone down in history as their rescuer, responsible for reuniting the Poe family after all those decades.

The truth is that Gill embellished the story. It was actually John Valentine, the owner of the vault Virginia was placed in, who went to check on his family's remains after hearing about the razing of the cemetery. He collected

Virginia's remains and reached out to the only person he knew locally that could figure out what to do with them: William Gill. For publicity, Gill fabricated a rescue story to make it sound like he was some big hero. On January 19, 1885 (the seventy-sixth anniversary of Edgar Allan Poe's birth), Virginia's remains were placed in a small bronze casket and interred to the left of her husband's. And so, the little family that struggled, laughed, loved, and endured life's wild storms together were now reunited for eternity.

─────── **LITERARY CONNECTIONS** ───────

In 1877, two years after the dedication of the monument that now stands nobly over the remains of Edgar Allan Poe, Virginia Poe, and Maria Clemm, Sara Rice (the woman responsible for making that monument happen) published *Edgar Allan Poe: A Memorial Volume*. The book contains a biographical sketch by John Ingram and letters from poets and authors such as John Greenleaf Whittier, Henry Wadsworth Longfellow, John Neal, and Sarah Helen Whitman. Also included in the volume are poetic tributes from Stéphane Mallarmé, Paul Hamilton Hayne, and Edgar Fawcett.

The Poe Toaster

Since around 1949 (or maybe even earlier), a mysterious figure that came to be known as the Poe Toaster has observed Edgar Allan Poe's birthday (January 19) with a unique ritual. Cloaked in darkness, wearing a wide-brimmed hat and a white scarf, the Toaster would scale the gates of Westminster Burying Ground. There, he would pay his respects at Poe's monument with a silent toast using a bottle of fine cognac, leaving the remainder at the monument as an offering. Along with the remaining cognac, the Toaster would leave behind three red roses, thought to be for Poe, his wife, and his mother-in-law. This peculiar tradition, first documented in 1950, would later captivate Jeff Jerome, curator of the Poe House and Museum in Baltimore.

From 1977 onward, Jerome, along with a growing group of onlookers, eagerly awaited the Toaster's arrival. They would watch from Westminster's catacombs or from the church through the entire night and early morning for a glimpse of the tall, shadowy figure. The Toaster, always maintaining his anonymity with his white scarf covering most of his face, would leave his tributes at the monument or the original gravesite, varying his approach based on the size of the crowd to stay as elusive as possible. His visits would often occur after midnight.

Over the years, the Toaster occasionally left notes, hinting at a plan for a successor to continue the tradition. One note in the 1990s stated that "the torch will be passed," with a subsequent note stating that the original Toaster had passed away and that a "son" would perform the annual toast. But following Poe's bicentennial in 2009, the Toaster failed to appear again. Jerome waited a few more years before he officially called the tradition over in 2012, leaving behind a mystery and a legacy of intrigue surrounding the enigmatic Poe Toaster.

THE MORE YOU KNOW

In 2016, the Maryland Historical Society sought to revive the Poe Toaster tradition by holding auditions for a successor. Jeff Jerome, while invited to judge the candidates, expressed reservations, concerned that a new interpretation might diminish the original's mystique. The chosen Toaster, adhering to the original's attire and cognac and roses tribute, added a couple of twists: a violin performance and a spoken Latin toast. The new tradition is conducted in broad daylight for public viewing. After seeing the audience's reaction, Jerome acknowledged that the revival had successfully captured the spirit of the original and agreed that it was the right way to go.

Poe's Hair

Some enduring mysteries like the identity of the Poe Toaster or the circumstances surrounding Poe's death may forever remain unsolved. However, this has not deterred attempts to unravel these mysteries. In 2006, a scientific investigation sought to shed light on Poe's demise by analyzing strands of his hair, meticulously preserved since his death in 1849 after they were cut from his head as keepsakes. Led by Albert Donnay, an environmental health engineer in Baltimore, the analysis aimed to identify potential causes of Poe's death or at least rule out certain possibilities. Given the disintegration of Poe's remains over the decades, his hair offered a unique opportunity to glean insights into his health.

The laboratory also analyzed hair samples from Virginia Poe, hoping to gain a broader understanding of the couple's living conditions. The tests revealed the presence of various toxic heavy metals, commonly found in nineteenth-century food, water, alcohol, medicines, and even gas lighting. This analysis could provide valuable clues about potential environmental exposures that may have contributed to Poe's ill health at the end of his life, which could account for his mysterious and untimely death. Or at the very least, it could rule out some of the theories of how he died.

No toxically high levels of metal were found in Poe's hair. Virginia's levels were much higher but still not enough to have contributed to her death. The levels, however, did change over time from the older to the newer ends of the hair strands. For example, Poe's mercury level increased over the course of a few months by more than 200 percent. This was likely due to the calomel he was prescribed when he had cholera in Philadelphia. This percentage was still significantly below the level associated with symptoms of mercury poisoning. While the percentages found of metals like arsenic, vanadium, uranium, nickel, and lead were higher than today's averages, none of the levels were high enough to have contributed significantly to the health of either Poe or Virginia.

─────── **THE MORE YOU KNOW** ───────

The analysis of Edgar Allan Poe's hair revealed a significant decline in lead levels during the final three to five months of his life. Given the high lead content in nineteenth-century alcohol and medicines, this suggests that Poe may have adhered to the temperance pledge he made to his fiancée during those last few months of his life. However, these findings can't definitively say whether or not alcohol played a role in his death, as hair doesn't rapidly absorb metals from the body in just the few days' time between when Poe was found until he died.

─────────── ───────────

Poe's Museums

Who hat literary figure has multiple museums, plaques, and gravestones? None other than Edgar Allan Poe! In fact, few historical figures have as many commemorations. Poe is arguably the most celebrated writer in America. With a total of four museums along the East Coast of the United States, fans from around the world travel to his many memorials to gain a closer insight into Poe's life and times.

In 1922, Richmond, Virginia, opened the first museum dedicated to Edgar Allan Poe. Housed within the city's oldest residence, the Old Stone House, the Poe Museum building doesn't have a direct connection to Poe. However, the writer grew up in the neighborhood and is known to have visited the house on at least one occasion in 1824 while escorting the Marquis de Lafayette as part of a junior honor color guard. The Poe Museum owns the foremost collection of artifacts and Poe's personal belongings.

LITERARY CONNECTIONS

Christopher P. Semtner, the curator of the Poe Museum in Richmond, Virginia, has published a number of books on Edgar Allan Poe. This includes *The Poe Shrine: Building the World's Finest Edgar Allan Poe Collection,* which delves into the evolution of the museum's ever-growing collection while doubling as a biography on the life of Edgar Allan Poe.

The second museum to open its doors, in 1949, was the Edgar Allan Poe House and Museum in Baltimore. It occupies the modest Amity Street rowhouse where Poe resided with his aunt, grandmother, and cousins. This intimate setting, where he spent his early years with the cousin who would become his wife, offers visitors a glimpse into Poe's life within his close-knit family.

In 1975, the cottage in the Bronx that was Poe's final residence was turned into a museum. Located in Poe Park, an oasis amid the bustling city, the Edgar Allan Poe Cottage lets fans peer into Poe's life in Fordham. The cottage even has the very bed Virginia died in, as a poignant reminder of the emotional ups and downs that Edgar Allan Poe experienced while living there. Finally, in 1980, the only surviving residence from Poe's time in Philadelphia opened as a museum under the operation of the National Park Service. All these museums remain open to the public today, offering a tangible connection to the life and times of the celebrated writer.

Poe's Legacy

Edgar Allan Poe's legacy and relevance transcend the nineteenth century, weaving through contemporary culture in countless ways. His works have been prolifically adapted, from classic films starring Vincent Price to more contemporary iterations like *The Simpsons'* take on "The Raven" and Mike Flanagan's Netflix series *The Fall of the House of Usher*. Poe even made an appearance on *South Park* as a sassy, moody ghost summoned by goth kids. He can truly be found in the most unexpected places!

But Poe's influence extends beyond the screen into many aspects of popular culture. His face adorns T-shirts and socks, while the Baltimore Ravens football team proudly bears the name of his iconic poem. Edgar Allan Poe has managed to stay relatable for centuries, a feat not many other writers from the nineteenth century have been able to achieve. His multifaceted legacy is partly the result of his inventing and pioneering genres beloved today. Many argue that Poe knew his audience better than they knew themselves, and in many ways, he set the bar for every writer and artist that came after him. It's hard *not* to find at least one element in a piece of writing, music, film, or art that can be traced back to Poe.

The Master of the Macabre continues to captivate audiences with his tales of terror and psychological suspense. His poetry rings in the minds of his readers (perhaps like the incessant utterings of a raven or the tolling of a bell . . .). His works are deeply ingrained in the collective consciousness and in culture, while scholars point to his biography as a timeless reminder of human endurance in the face of adversity. Edgar Allan Poe's life was plagued by tragedy and hardship, but despite his struggles, his literary achievements would be celebrated and studied for generations to come. His greatest testaments include not just his literary masterpieces but also the enduring passion of his fans, who ensure his legacy lives on—forevermore.

LITERARY CONNECTIONS

As if Edgar Allan Poe's literary footprint was not prevalent enough, he has become the name and face of a literary award. The Mystery Writers of America hosts an annual ceremony that features the Edgar Awards, statuettes of the man himself. The awards are presented to the best in mystery fiction, nonfiction, television, film, and theater.

Further Reading

- *A Mystery of Mysteries: The Death and Life of Edgar Allan Poe.* By Mark Dawidziak. St. Martin's Press, an imprint of St. Martin's Publishing Group—In this biography, Dawidziak explores Poe's life beginning with his death, captivating readers with a double-timeline narrative.
- *Edgar Allan Poe's Tales of Mystery and Madness* and *Edgar Allan Poe's Tales of Death and Dementia.* Illustrated by Gris Grimly. Atheneum Books for Young Readers—These abridged editions of select works by Poe are accompanied by some beautifully weird art by Gris Grimly.
- *Poe's Helen Remembers.* Edited by John Carl Miller. University Press of Virginia—This compilation of letters between Poe's fiancée Sarah Helen Whitman and early biographer John Henry Ingram reveal more about the correspondents than about the subject. A fascinating read for die-hard fans of Poe.
- *The Collected Letters of Edgar Allan Poe* (in two volumes). Edited by John Ward Ostrom, Burton R. Pollin, and Jeffrey A. Savoye. Gordian Press—The most comprehensive collection of Poe's letters, save those that have been discovered after 2008.
- *The Collected Works of Edgar Allan Poe* (in three volumes, 1969 and 1978 editions). Edited by Thomas Ollive

Mabbott. The Belknap Press of Harvard University Press—The definitive collection of Poe's works, most frequently quoted by Poe scholars.

- *The Final Days of Edgar Allan Poe: Nevermore in Baltimore.* By David F. Gaylin. Lehigh University Press—The facts of Poe's mysterious death have long been subject to fabrication, distortion, and inaccuracy. Gaylin has compiled an exhaustive and definitive account of everything known about Poe's demise.

- *The Poe Log: A Documentary Life of Edgar Allan Poe 1809–1849.* By Dwight Thomas and David K. Jackson. G.K. Hall & Co.—A compilation of facts about Poe's life, recording nearly every day of it.

- *The Poe Shrine: Building the World's Finest Edgar Allan Poe Collection.* By Christopher P. Semtner. America Through Time, an imprint of Fonthill Media—This book was written by the curator of the Poe Museum in Richmond, Virginia. It's a discovery of Poe's life and the people in his circle through the artifacts comprising the museum's foremost collection.

- *Who Was Edgar Allan Poe?* By Jim Gigliotti. Illustrated by Tim Foley. Penguin Workshop, an imprint of Penguin Random House—Part of the Who Was? series, this book does a fantastic job giving a brief yet accurate introduction to Poe. Recommended for children, young adults, or adults who want an easy read about Poe's life.

Index

About the Author

LEVI LIONEL LELAND is a born-and-raised Rhode Islander with a near lifelong passion for Edgar Allan Poe and his works. After visiting every Poe museum and house in the country, he focused his attention homeward, learning all he could about Poe's time in Providence, and creating the *Edgar Allan Poe: Rhode Island* website and A Walking Tour of Poe's Providence, where he shares his research and passion for our favorite gothic poet.

About the Illustrator

KIM ARRINGTON is an artist and illustrator living in Birmingham, Alabama. She primarily paints in watercolor and gouache, and sketches with ink, graphite, and colored pencils, creating loose and whimsically detailed images. Her simple joys in life are reading, drinking coffee, gardening, traveling, sketching, and spending time with her husband and four daughters.